MORE WHISTLES

Martyn Gilchrist

Published in 2005 by Martyn Gilchrist
'More Whistles'
PO Box 3841, Wincanton, BA9 8WX, UK

First published 2005
ISBN 0 9550231 0 6
British Library Cataloguing in Publication Data.
A catalogue record for this book is available from the British Library.

Title page: *TOP ROW l. to r. Military whistle '2 BKS', 2nd Berkshire Regiment, early 20th century; J Hudson & Co round whistle, 1890s; W Dowler & Sons Beaufort whistle, 19th century; A De Courcy & Co Beaufort whistle pre 1927; J Dixon & Sons Beaufort whistle with ivory mouthpiece, 'Swaine & Co London', 19th century; J Hudson & Co multi-tube whistle, 1950s; B Lilly & Sons siren, 1910s; CENTRE ROW l. to r. probably H A Ward multi-tube whistle, 1900s; J Hudson & Co general service whistle military issue, '↑1 1902'; J Hudson & Co general service whistle 'KCMHBH', Kent County Mental Hospital Barming Heath, where the word 'barmy' came from, early 1920s; J Hudson & Co hallmarked silver general service whistle 'Martyn Gilchrist', presented to the author by the company; S Auld escargot whistle 'S Auld's Improved Call Maker Glasgow', c.1890; J Hudson & Co composite whistle 'J Morris & Sons Manchester', fire equipment suppliers, 1890s; J Hudson & Co siren on leather wristlet, 1910s; BOTTOM ROW l. to r. A De Courcy & Co escargot 'GWR 18492 PW Dept', Great Western Railway Permanent Way Department, pre 1927; J Hudson & Co escargot 'The Officer's Call No.3', 1920s; J Hudson & Co escargot 'LT', London Transport dark green Bakelite 1930s; C T Willet escargot 'CTW's Rouser', 1920s-30s; J Hudson & Co escargot 'AG &CoS Startler' 1920s.*

NOTICE
The information contained in this book is accurate to the best of the author's knowledge. The author and publisher disclaim all liability associated with the use of any of this information.

ACKNOWLEDGEMENT
The author would like to thank Alan Kipping for allowing numerous whistles to be photographed for reproduction here, and to Hilary Griffiths for reading the manuscript and suggesting a number of improvements.

NOTE ON THE CAPTIONS & TEXT
Many patterns of whistles have been made for a considerable number of years, often decades. The dates given in the captions refer explicitly to the whistles illustrated. In references to dates, '1900s' indicates the years 1900 to 1909. It is not used to specify the 19th century generally. This style for centuries is used throughout the book.

Printed in Great Britain by Salisbury Printing Co Ltd
Greencroft Street
Salisbury SP1 1JF

Contents

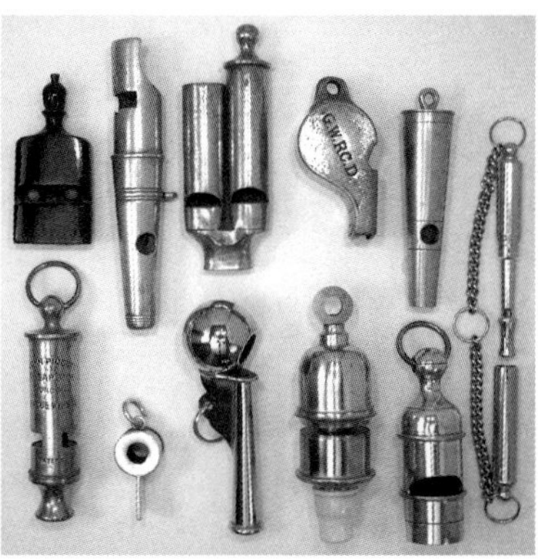

Types of whistles. TOP ROW, *left to right: (1) multi-chambered whistle, two chambers within the body. J Hudson & Co, 1900s, horn. (2) composite or double-ended whistle. Two whistles joined top-to-top. J Hudson & Co, notched window, 1890s-1900s, nickel silver, length 100mm. (3) multi-tube whistle, two tubes joined to a single mouthpiece. Nickel plated brass. (4) escargot – snail-like in appearance when viewed from the side. J Hudson & Co, 1920s, nickel plated brass. 'GWRCD', Great Western Railway Carriage Department. (5) Beaufort whistle. A tapered tube, the smallest end being placed in the mouth. A high quality nickel silver pattern by J Dixon & Sons, 1880s. (6) 'Silent' dog whistle with variable pitch. It can be adjusted by turning the end which has the effect of moving a rod inside the body up or down, thus altering the pitch. Made from 1935 onwards, the one illustrated is modern with a plastic fipple.*

BOTTOM ROW, *left to right: (1) general service whistle (GSW). J Hudson & Co, 1910s. 'John Piggott Ltd Cheapside London League Whistle'. GSW has been chosen to avoid confusion which may occur if describing a call of this type as a 'police whistle' when it is only intended to describe a shape and not a whistle issued to the police. (2) skeleton whistle. Special type of escargot whistle which has open barrel-ends. William Thornhill, hallmarked silver, 1879. (3) Swiss/French railways pattern. J Hudson & Co, 1940s-50s. (4) high quality bell whistle in lacquered brass with ivory mouthpiece. Stevens & Son 1860s, (5) round 'pea' whistle. T Yates, late 19th century.*

Introduction

A whistle is classed as an aerophone, which is an instrument in which sound is produced by vibrating air. The breath is directed at a sharp edge which sets the air in motion. The length of whistle's body governs the pitch and its shape the character of the sound.

Between the 1860s and the late 1930s many makers producing a wide range of patterns came and went, perhaps this was the 'Golden Age' of whistle making. Before 1860 little is known, and after the 1939-45 conflict came many changes including the steady downturn in the manufacture of different patterns of whistles.

In recent years collectors have shown great interest in the subject and the legacy that whistle manufacturers have left with the large number of different calls that have been produced. Models by the smaller makers are particularly scarce and often rare, as many of them were manufacturing only for a few years. Examples by some of the larger makers such as T Yates, J Dixon & Sons, W Dowler & Sons and A De Courcy & Co can all be very hard to find as by the twenty-first century they had not made whistles for many years. The splendid whistles by Stevens & Sons were made from at least the 1840s until the beginning of the twentieth century and most are now rare. Many early calls by J Hudson & Co are also scarce or rare.

Whistles have been used in many fields of human endeavour. When considering two particular spheres, the railways and the sports community, many people on hearing the phrase 'guard's whistle' or 'referee whistle' will conjure up in their mind's eye a call whose shape, when viewed from the side is reminiscent of a snail. This particular type of call is classified as an escargot whistle, from the French word meaning a snail.

Their use in sport, together with the multi-chambered pealess whistle, is almost universal. In the past this was not so. Referees were free to choose any model of whistle they liked, and formerly might single out patterns which are seen rarely in twenty-first century sport. For example, hockey umpires favoured in particular the multi-tube whistle with the distinctive tone it produced. Railway guards now prefer the escargot whistle but, as in sport, a number of different types have been used in the past. Both groups have used general service whistles (police-type calls), round pea whistles and Beaufort whistles and several other types to a lesser extent.

City and town public transport departments, including tramways, buses and London Underground, have all preferred the escargot, sometimes made with additional strengthening components designed to meet the rigorous conditions. Whistles at one time or another have been advertised as suitable for particular groups such as cyclists, the Scouts and Guides, night watchmen, and for dogs, high pitched calls.

Sirens are often of interest to the whistle collector. A chapter specifically covers the pattern, and it's derivatives, most frequently met with, J Hudson & Co's Model 147. They have been advertised as excellent for cyclists, motor cyclists, with or without a side car, as a motor horn, for yachtsmen and as a sound effects instrument. Sound is produced by air escaping through the holes of a rotating perforated wheel, the rotor, and the pitch varies with the speed of rotation.

Escargot whistles

The escargot whistle, which emerged sometime during the nineteenth century, is so called because of its snail-like shape when viewed from the side. It is the well-known whistle used by sports referees, umpires and railway guards. The basic design is a mouthpiece set at a tangent to a barrel or drum-like chamber containing a 'pea'. Maybe the earliest examples did once actually contain a dried pea but generally it is a cork ball, or more recently a ball of a synthetic material. Whistles containing a pea were at one time called 'self-tipping', this being a reference to the musical term 'tipping'. It is a way of manipulating the tongue so as to produce staccato effects from such instruments as the trumpet or flute—a pea whistle produces a similar effect. Without a pea the whistle will work perfectly well but without a staccato effect. Before inserting a cork pea into the barrel it must first be steamed to make it pliable enough to be squeezed through the window without damage.

'Thunderer' is a word sometimes used to describe this particular type of whistle and is found on many old examples made by a number of manufacturers. Before 1927 it was a common word for an escargot with no one company being able to claim its exclusive use. From 23rd December 1927 it became the trademark of J Hudson & Co after several court cases spanning a number of years. Strictly speaking, from that time 'Thunderer' has meant patterns made by J Hudson & Co and not a particular design of whistle. The phrases 'London escargot' and 'Glasgow escargot' are used here to describe the two styles of whistle into which the various patterns conveniently fall, see illustration.

The two styles of escargots. Left; London escargot, made by C T Willets. Right; Glasgow escargot, made by S Auld.

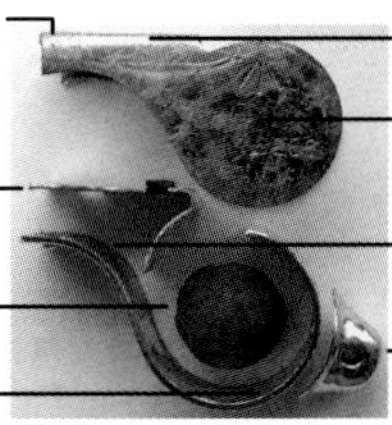

The London escargot, includes the early patterns which often employed the use of buttons, similar to those which were sewn on to the front or sleeve of tunics. They were also, and still are, make from appropriately shaped metal blanks pressed out of sheet metal, and then bent and soldered together. Rumour has it that escargots of this type, marked London 'Thunderer', were being made before volume producers came into existence.

The Glasgow escargot, developed as follows. Many button whistles have an under-strengthening piece which is attached inside the front of the mouthpiece and then curves downwards towards the barrel where it is soldered. An open triangular area is left between the under-strengthening and the whistle. If the under-strengthening is replaced with a component which fills the open area then the result would be a highly robust call. This pattern was achieved by S Auld of Glasgow, using six components, with the design being registered on 29th January 1890, number 143091. One of the components was a solid metal casting which had the effect of filling in the triangular area described above. An important design consideration was the prevention of the pea from being propelled towards the mouthpiece and jamming, but with Auld's solid casting this was impossible. Later designs, often patented, did not use castings but instead constructed escargots from components stamped out of metal sheeting. The pea was prevented from jamming by the use of a tongue inside the whistle. This is a suitably shaped piece of metal which is soldered inside the floor of the mouthpiece, and proceeds along the inside to the barrel where it curves downwards. This effectively blanks off the hollow triangular area thus preventing the pea from entering this region.

The Glasgow whistle is the most difficult escargot to manufacture but it is also the most robust. Some have been made with additional strengthening pieces applied to the barrel ends making them physically one of the strongest whistles ever made. Whistles constructed in a way similar to Auld's were made by Peter McDonald, Glasgow, and Authur Ward, Birmingham. Jointly they applied for a patent which appears in the records as number 2980, 25th February 1890—less than a month after Auld's registered design. This patent application was abandoned. Whistles made by McDonald are probable the rarest of all Glasgow escargots followed by those of Ward. Other manufacturers soon started patenting and marketing their own models: J Hudson & Co's first patent for this pattern was 19868/1891, R A Walton sold 'The Roller' from about 1901 (no examples of this call are known), A De Courcy & Co's first patent was 26019/1905 and C F Gaunt 22309/1911 (no examples of this call are known).

BUTTON WHISTLES

Button escargot whistles have been made from the nineteenth century, their basic design constituting the earliest type of escargot call. Also included in this category are coin whistles. It is a myth that somehow none of them are 'official' or 'genuine' and that they were all made up by enthusiasts and are, one way or another, not 'proper' whistles. The vast majority are genuine escargots, authorised by the concerns whose buttons have been utilised. However, it is true that a very small minority have been made by keen individuals, and during the late twentieth century some have been made up with commerce in mind.

The buttons used were of both single-piece and two-piece construction with the shank, through which the button-thread would normally go, being removed. The button makers name can generally be seen by looking inside the whistle.

Left; single-piece button, C & J Weldon, London. Right; two-piece button A J Robbins, London, diameter 26mm.

When employing two-piece buttons, the back may, or may not, have been removed. In traditional button whistles a strip of metal was bent around the two buttons to form the barrel of an escargot. The metal strip, after completing all but about a tenth of the way round, would be bent outwards so that its direction was almost at a tangent to the barrel. It continued for a short distance before being terminated. Around this protruding strip would be bent and soldered a further piece of tin plate to form the mouthpiece. Often the width of the mouthpiece is less at the window than at the front. Nearly all of these whistles have an additional metal understrengthening piece which is attached inside the front of the mouthpiece. It then proceeds towards the barrel where it is soldered. The strip continues around the barrel and finally turns over to form a short tube suitable to take a wire loop, often triangular, for a lanyard.

Various makers, for example, Gaunts and Hudsons, advertised that they could manufacture button whistles. In actuality, some of Hudson's earliest factory production escargots look like button whistles. Button whistles could be a customer's answer to having only a few whistles made which sported an organisation's identity at a reasonable cost. The alternative was having to pay for a hand cut punch with which to mark whistles, an option which has never been cheap. As well as escargots, buttons have also been attached to general service, Beaufort and other whistle patterns. They have been divided up into four groups as described below.

Group 1. Aristocrats, institutions and companies had whistles made with tunic-front or, more rarely, the smaller sleeve buttons. They mostly bear an organisations' crest, badge or monogram, though there were some which were plain. They were made by whistle manufacturers, and by craftsmen, at a time when there were many firms able to make such items to a high standard, including railway company workshops. In this group it is convenient to place factory made button whistles where the buttons are attached to standard production escargots.

Group 1. Left to right: Staffordshire Constabulary buttons affixed by J Hudson & Co to one of their escargots, c.1890; Military service buttons; Customs; livery sleeve buttons of Duncan of Ardounie; Hertfordshire Police, length 50mm.

Group 1. Left to right: London & North Western Railway; Lancashire & Yorkshire Railway; Bank of England, length 47mm; Great Eastern Railway; York Castle.

Group 2. Coin whistles in which coins instead of buttons have been used.

Right: *Group 2. Coin whistles. Left; George V half-penny. One side obverse, the other reverse with coin dated 1919. Right; farthings , one Victoria, the other Edward VII.*

Left: *Group 2. Coin whistles. Made by Thornhill & Co, London, Hallmarked silver using 1887 shillings, commemorating Queen Victoria's golden jubilee.*

Group 3. A catch-all group to include those button, coin and badge escargots which do not fit into the other groups. This group is for those put together by individuals whose only desire perhaps was to have such a whistle, with no intention to pass off or commercially sell the escargot. Some used production escargots to which a badge or coin was affixed, others were constructed in a more traditional way. The latter type can, by and large, be quickly discerned as the workmanship does not match that of an artisan and/or the style is completely individual.

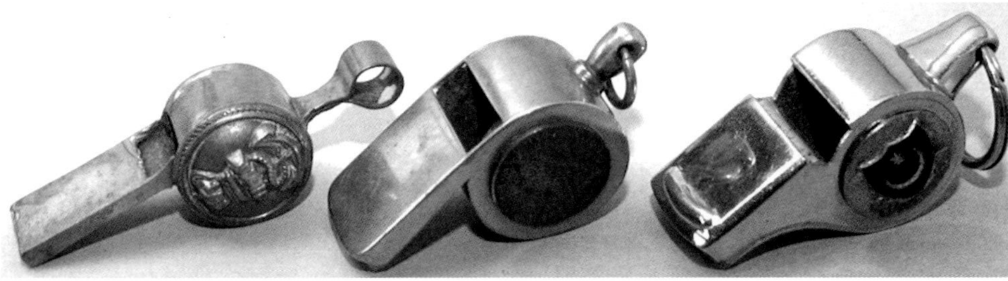

Group 3. Button whistles that do not fit into any other group. Left to right: naval button; Queen Victoria farthing attached one side, Edward VII farthing the other; crest of Southsea, Hampshire attached to a 1920s A De Courcy & Co largest size escargot.

Group 4. Button whistles where two-piece buttons have been soldered to factory made escargots at a later date for the purpose of supplying the tourist, novelty or collectors' market. The buttons are not flush with the whistle but thrust out from the side. Made towards the end of the twentieth century using old and brand-new calls. They would not have been employed or officially ordered by the concerns whose buttons have been used.

Group 4. Specious button whistles. Two-piece buttons soldered to both old and new escargots, late 20th century. Dublin United Tramways (DUT) and regimental buttons.

SKELETON WHISTLES

An unusual escargot is the skeleton whistle which has the barrel entirely open at both sides. It can be sounded when the fingers are placed over the ends thus creating an effective resonating chamber. One style was patented by Mersch & Dold, 1594/1887, and over the years it has been made by numerous concerns including silversmiths. Some are of rudimentary construction and others of a more advanced design, probably intended as a watch-chain whistle.

Skeleton whistles. Left; a basic design manufactured by a number of companies, this example silver and unmarked, length 30mm. Centre & right; sophisticated silver models made by the London silversmith William Thornhill, both hallmarked for 1879.

ADIE BROS

Adie Brothers, Birmingham made a single pattern of Glasgow escargot. They were probably contracted by the government to do so as the result of J Hudson & Co premises being damaged by a direct hit from a high-explosive bomb which blew up in the factory's basement in October 1940.

Left: *Adie Bros. Mouthpiece marked 'Adie Bros Birmingham 1941 ↑', loop stamped 'PAD'. Nickel silver with a brass tongue, barrel-end diameter 28mm.*

Right: *S Auld & Co. 'Improved Call', Registered Design 143091/1890.*

S AULD & CO

Samuel Auld designed the Glasgow escargot, a very robust whistle, made in three sizes using six components. In May 1907, and trading from 54 Cowcaddens, Glasgow, they sold to J Hudson & Co their whistle business. This included their large stock of whistles, goodwill, tools and the right for Hudsons to use the name S Auld. Hudsons were still selling in the 1920s Auld's Glasgow whistles which were probably part of the stock they had acquired. Almost certainly Aulds 1890 design would not be made in the 1920s having been superseded by Hudson's own more modern patterns.

S Auld & Co. View showing how the whistle was constructed from a number of pieces and the distinctive ridge across the underside of the barrel.

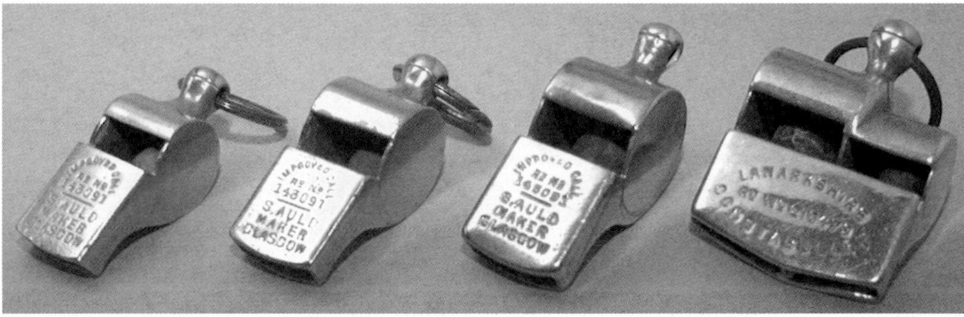

S Auld & Co. 'The Improved Call' made in three sizes, as illustrated, Registered Design 143091, 29th January 1890. Right; an extraordinary double escargot, Registered Design 210479/1893. The mouthpiece is divided into two and the front edge is 'V' shaped, This enables either of the whistles to be blown individually or both together, width 38mm. Marked 'Lanarkshire Constabulary' on the mouthpiece and '295' on the largest barrel-end. Very rare.

B & H WHISTLES

William Hussy of Hockley, Birmingham made escargots between 1969 and 1972 and marked his whistle 'The Hustler'. He was bought out by M Y Dart Co (Games) Ltd who continued to make whistles to Hussy's design but marked them with the trademark 'Halex'.

B & H Whistles. all marked on the mouthpiece 'The Hustler Regd Made In England'. Back left; large size, chrome plated, barrel-end diameter 25mm. Back right; large tapered model with finger grips. Front left; small tapered model with strengthening side plates, unplated brass. Front right; small tapered model.

J BARRALL

John Barrall traded in Birmingham between 1886 and 1898. His London escargots are rare and there may well be further models in addition to those illustrated.

John Barrall 1886-98. Some calls were marked on the top of the mouthpiece 'Barrall Birmingham' within an ellipse.

J Barrall. Left & centre left; marked with the Salvation Army crest. The crest is almost *the same as those used on Hudson whistles. J Barrall and J Hudson & Co almost certainly had the same specialist toolmakers to cut the punches used to mark whistles. Nickel plated brass, barrel-end diameters 23mm & 24mm. Centre right & right; marked on the mouthpiece top within an ellipse 'Barrall Birmingham'. All rare.*

BLACK & CO

Black & Co of Glasgow was the company that made London escargots for McPherson brothers, Glasgow, between 1888 and 1898. From 1899 McPhersons ordered the more sturdy Glasgow escargot from Hudsons.

Black & Co, Glasgow, 'The Thunderer'.

Black & Co. Left; marked above the window in a rectangular frame 'The Thunderer', below the window '↑ C.G.R.', Cape Government Railway, and backstamped 'McPherson Brothers Makers 156 Argyle St Glasgow'. Barrel-end diameter 26mm. Right; marked above the window in a rectangular frame 'The Thunderer' and below the window 'McPherson Brothers Makers 156 Argyle St Glasgow'. Rare.

Cascelloid Ltd. The barrel-end of the whistle is marked 'Palitoy Regd Made In England' and moulded inside 'CAS'. Orange plastic, barrel-end diameter 29mm. Rare.

CASCELLOID LTD

In the late 1940s Cascelloid manufactured under licence from J Hudson & Co, escargot whistles made to their Patent 447673 of 1936 (the patent's valid period expired in 1952). The whistle is made from two interlocking halves which are held together by two eyelets. One eyelet is located at the top, the other to the rear of the mouthpiece at the base.

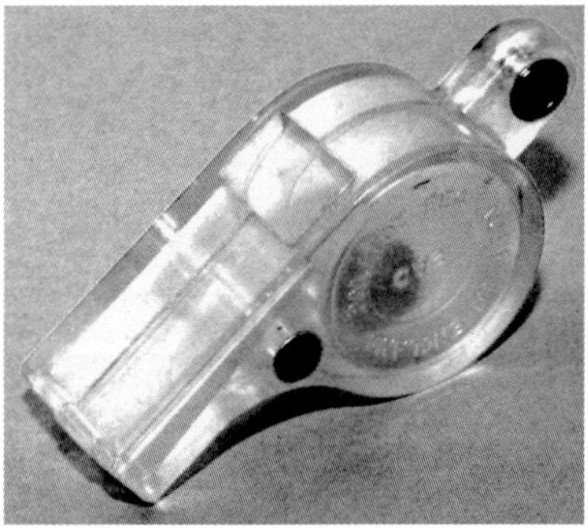

ALFRED DE COURCY & CO

A De Courcy manufactured a number of escargots, some of them patented. The company used several styles of top fitting, three of them being exclusive to their calls. These provide a convenient feature with which to identify those calls which are not marked with his name. They made whistles for sports companies, the government, railways and various commercial and retail businesses.

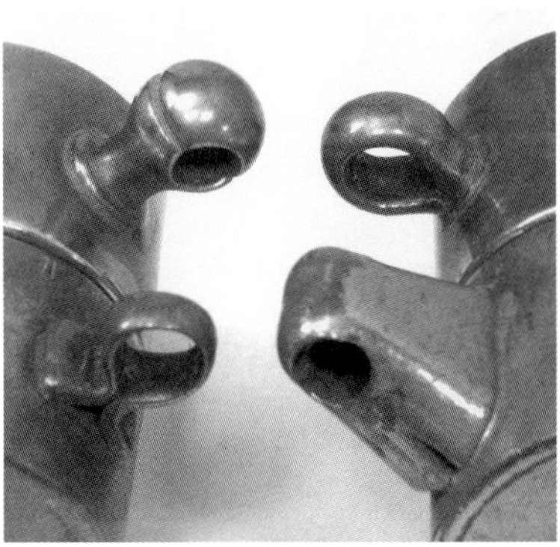

A De Courcy & Co top fittings. All are exclusive to the company except the one at top-left. They are a reliable feature for identification purposes. Top-right; a looped wire pushed into the body. Bottom left; a wire, distinctively shaped and pushed through the body. Bottom right; a hollow 'V' formed from a folded over blank.

A De Courcy's first patent for a Glasgow escargot dates from 1905, number 26019. Whistles were constructed from four pressings plus a top fitting. One pressing making a complete side and incorporating half of the top of the mouthpiece, a second mirror-image piece for the other side. A third piece was soldered inside the mouthpiece at the top to hold pieces one and two together, and finally a piece curved round to form the barrel and base of the mouthpiece. No examples of this call are known.

A De Courcy & Co. Glasgow escargots were made in three sizes. All are marked on the mouthpiece 'The Thunderer Patent'. 'Patent' relates to De Courcy's second patent, number 824, valid from 1907 to 1921, and these calls are the ones most frequently met with. They are made from three pieces plus a top fitting. One blank is bent to form both sides and the top of the mouthpiece, a second blank is curved to make the barrel and bottom of the mouthpiece, and the third blank is the tongue which goes from inside the front of the mouthpiece to the back and curves down into the barrel. Its purpose is to stop the 'pea' jamming. This construction looks similar to Hudson's patent whistle except in one particular. That is, in De Courcy's design the tongue slid into grooves cut into the inside of the barrel-ends but only vestiges of this feature are sometimes visible after the whistle has been assembled. Left; smallest size, top marked 'B.C.T', a town's corporation transport department. Barrel-end diameter 21mm. Centre left; medium size, barrel-end diameter 24mm. Centre right; largest size, 'Henry Riley, Constitution Hill, Birmingham'. One barrel-end marked 'G.C.R', Great Central Railway, the other 'P Way 1658', Permanent Way, barrel-end diameter 27mm. Right; largest size, marked 'L & N.E.R', London & North Eastern Railway.

Above: *A De Courcy & Co. Left; military London escargot made to Patent 122572 of 1918. Top of the mouthpiece marked 'A De Courcy & Co Birmingham Patent Pending 1918' and a barrel-end hand marked '↑'. A metal blank is formed to make the two sides and the mouthpiece top, a second, the barrel and mouthpiece base. It is distinctive by having the edges of the body bent over the barrel-ends. Plated steel, barrel-end diameter 27mm. Right; large Glasgow escargot, c.1910s-20s embossed on both barrel-ends with a hand logo and the words 'Trade Mark'. Reading down the whistle, 'Suter Hartmann & Rahtjen's Composition Co Ltd London'. The company were suppliers to shipping companies of anti-fouling compositions and paints. A handsome whistle that would have been expensive to produce.*

Right: *A De Courcy & Co. Left; Patent 122572/1918 showing how the body edges are bent over the barrel-end. Right; The illustration shows how the mouthpiece is formed from a separate top piece which is soldered and held by folded over tabs to the bottom of the mouthpiece. Whistles can also be found of the same construction without tabs*

Below: *A De Courcy & Co. London light gauge escargots made in three sizes with end-cap diameters of 19mm, 23mm & 27mm. Left; mouthpiece marked 'Sports Ltd High Street Leicester'. Centre left & right; end-caps have concentric circles, top of the mouthpiece is held to the bottom by folded over tabs. Right; mouthpiece marked 'Referee'.*

Above: *A De Courcy & Co London escargots. Left; tapered mouthpiece, one barrel-end marked 'Abbey', the other 'Cyclone', 21mm. Abbey is a sports company. Right; small size with domed barrel-ends, 19mm. Underside of barrel marked 'A De Courcy & Co', rare.*

Above: *A De Courcy & Co. The company sold to J Hudson & Co in 1927 their whistle making business including the remaining stock. Hudson buffed off De Courcy's markings where possible and added their own. Illustrated are two such very rare whistles. Left; almost a Glasgow escargot – it is a London escargot with an additional small solid brass piece between the mouthpiece and barrel. Top marked 'Mitchell Manchester', backstamp 'The Acme Registered J.H & Co Birmm'. Right; London escargot, back stamp 'The Thunderer Registered'. Hudson unsuccessfully pursued through the courts for many years the registration of 'Thunderer' as a trademark. After the purchase of De Courcy's whistle business their application succeeded.*

A De Courcy & Co. Side view of the whistle depicted in the previous illustration, on the left, showing the small solid piece between mouthpiece and barrel.

J R GAUNT & SON

J R Gaunt devised an escargot made from two pieces of sheet metal, Patent 22309/1911. Examples of this call are unknown.

J HUDSON & CO

J Hudson & Co have made many different patterns of London and Glasgow escargot whistles in several qualities in both metal and plastic for many years. The descriptions of their numerous patterns have been divided into three groups; metal London, metal Glasgow and plastic Glasgow.

METAL LONDON ESCARGOTS

Hudson's first escargot whistles, London whistles, date from 1884 but there are no positively identified examples from this year. However, in 1886 the trademark 'The Acme' was registered and calls reminiscent of button whistles and marked 'The Acme' do exist and were probably made from around this time.

Originally, buttons used for whistles were either one-piece and did not have a rim, or two-piece with a rim. The curved brass strip that formed the barrel of the whistle did not have any predetermined position to locate to, but was simply soldered to the buttons. In Hudson's early escargots, what would have been the button at each end of the barrel was instead a cap with a narrow rim at right angles to the edge within which seated firmly the soldered curved brass strip that formed the barrel. The strip after going all the way round inside the cap, except for the amount of circumference required to be left open for the window, was bent outwards at almost a tangent to the barrel. It continued for a short distance before being terminated. Around this protruding tangential strip would be bent and soldered a further piece to make the mouthpiece.

J Hudson & Co. Rare London escargots from the mid 1880s, top of the mouthpieces marked 'The Acme Registered J H & Co Birmm', wider at the front than at the window. An under-strengthening piece curves from the front of the mouthpiece to the base of the barrel, and continues to almost the back where it rolls over to form a narrow tube through which is placed a wire loop to take a lanyard. End-caps left to right; bicycle wheel, plain, mounted penny-farthing bicycle. A further design exists from this period, a dog's head. This last design continued to be used on various standard models for at least a further thirty-five years.

Registered Design 230905 of 1894. The main feature was a parallel sided mouthpiece with tooth-grips to the top and bottom of large size models, and just to the top for small models. The mouthpiece was made from a metal strip shaped to form a box which slid over the tongue—the tongue extended backwards and curved round, becoming the barrel of the whistle. End-caps with a location groove for the mouthpiece were added, plus a hollow spherical knop. A cork 'pea' was inserted to complete the whistle. Escargots were made to this configuration in four sizes and being of a light construction were inexpensive. As time went by various designs were applied to the end caps. An early change was the omission of a tooth-grip to the underside of the mouthpiece. Whistles continued to be made to the fundamental design until 1924 when Patent 214519 (lodged on 19th July 1923) specified a more advanced construction. The top fitting was shaped as a winged 'V' with the 'wings' locating in grooves in the end-caps. This location groove, with that for the mouthpiece, guaranteed the correct relative position of top fitting to mouthpiece. On whistles made from this date onwards that have another type of fitting the location grooves can often be see at the shoulder of the whistle. The winged 'V' fitting continued for many years and was attached to many different types of whistle.

Left: *J Hudson & Co Patent 214519/1924, winged 'V' top fitting.*

Right; *J Hudson & Co. Left; mouthpiece construction of inexpensive London escargots from 1894 until the last few decades of the 20th century. Right; last mouthpiece design on London escargots before being discontinued in the 1970s.*

By the late 1930s only the two small sizes were available, made with plain barrel-ends. Sometime during the 1939-45 conflict choice was further reduced leaving only the smallest model. However, the medium sized call reappeared a few years later until both were discontinued in the 1970s. At the time of cancellation the mouthpiece construction differed from the one that had been used since the 1890s (see the illustration on the previous page).

J Hudson & Co London escargots. Left; small model, 1950s-60s, barrel-end diameter 20mm. Centre left; medium size model from the last period of manufacture in the 1970s. Top of the mouthpiece attached by turning over tabs onto the bottom component which continues backwards to form the barrel, barrel-end diameter 21mm. Centre right; medium size with winged 'V' top fitting locating in grooves in the end-caps. 'Patent 214519/24' - in 1924 patents were valid for 16 years. Right; largest size with Registered Design number 230905 marked on the mouthpiece. The design dates from 1894 and was valid for five years, barrel-end diameter 26mm, made in four sizes.

J Hudson & Co London escargot from the 1940s with an under-strengthening piece – an 'antique' style for this date. Top of mouthpiece marked 'LMS', London Midland & Scottish Railway.

In the early 1930s appeared cheap escargots of light construction, their mouthpieces formed by a shaped metal strip clipped and soldered to either side of the tongue. The tongue itself became the bottom of the mouthpiece. In Hudson's other patterns the tongue was completely enclosed by a box-shaped strip which created the mouthpiece, the tongue only being visible by looking inside the mouthpiece.

J Hudson & Co London escargots made in four sizes, with the end-caps embossed 'The Acme England' around the edge. In the centre a 'J H & Co' monogram. Barrel-end diameters 20mm, 23mm, 25mm & 27mm, mid 1920s-40s.

J Hudson & Co London escargots with end-caps figuring a rose, shamrock & thistle. Their relative Registered Design numbers of 1911 are 576579, 578510 & 577844. The designs are symbolic of England, Ireland and Scotland. A further design for a Tudor rose was lodged but it is believed none were ever produced. The whistles illustrated have been chosen to show how their features changed over the years, the earliest on the left, the latest on the right. Left; rose, the top of the mouthpiece is marked 'Rose', the end-caps are marked with the Registered Design number, the top fitting is a knop. The first shamrock and thistle calls were marked in a similar way. Centre; the top of the mouthpiece is not marked with the name of the design, however, the end-caps bear the design number and the top, a winged 'V', is made to Patent 214519 and this number is marked above the window. Right; the mouthpiece is not marked with the design's name, nor is there a design number on the end-caps and the top fitting is a cap without a groove, typical of the 1940s.

J Hudson & Co London escargot made for the toy market. Top fitting a winged 'V', with the wings hidden inside the barrel, tin plate, barrel-end diameter 28mm. Largest size, two smaller sizes were also made.

J Hudson & Co were first allowed a patent for a metal London escargot with a parallel sided mouthpiece in 1897, number 19640, and at that date patents were valid for fourteen years. For the life of the patent, up to 1911, whistles were marked 'Patent', usually on the underside of the mouthpiece. Sometimes escargots are found marked 'Patent' beyond this date. Perhaps an obsolete component was used or maybe they were marked in error. The 1897 patent specified a whistle made from two pieces plus a top fitting. One blank is bent to form the circular barrel-ends, the mouthpiece top and sides. The other blank is a strip which is curved to make the barrel and then bent at an angle to form the base of the mouthpiece. They were made in four sizes until the mid 1940s when all were discontinued. The front edge of the smallest escargot is straight and not curved as in the other sizes. Any of them could be fitted with a leather wrist-strap, Patent 25619/1907, and metal finger-grips were also available. The smallest size was made with a compass set into a barrel-end from the 1910s to the 1920s, and to the other three sizes from the 1910s to the mid 1940s.

Put together in the 1930s were patterns made entirely of nickel plated zinc. Few of these seem to have survived, perhaps because the whistle retains little appeal when the plating wears away to reveal the zinc beneath. During the 1940s and 1950s a cheap range fabricated from thin gauge sheeting was made. They were made in three sizes, the two largest being hard to find.

Further variations to the basic calls were as follows. In 1908 Patent 10898 specified additional metal caps to be fitted to the barrel-ends and a metal strip, or wire, to go completely round the end of the mouthpiece. These two extras increased the strength of the whistle enormously and became popular with city transport companies. Often examples can be found with the caps but without the additional mouthpiece band. They were made in three sizes until the early 1940s. One strengthening cap for the medium sized call featured a dog's head, a pressing that had been used since the 19th century. As well as having the usual styles of top they can also be found with a loop similar to those used on general service whistles. This loop was a Registered Design, number 571315 of October 1910.

A variation to the second to largest basic model during the 1920s and 1930s was a modification whereby a curved lip extended beyond the bottom of the mouthpiece, thus aiding its retention in the mouth. This whistle is rare. A new model was launched in the 1960s; a small escargot with a long mouthpiece with extended lips to the top and bottom of the mouthpiece—this whistle is still made in the 2000s.

Above: *J Hudson & Co London escargots. Left; smallest size,'The Acme Thunderer', marked with the crest of the Salvation Army. Made between 1897 and 1911, barrel-end diameter 19mm. Centre left; One barrel-end marked 'Spratt's Patent' with a logo, the other with a dog's head. Centre right; the smallest model of Hudson's standard range, late 1920s, barrel-end diameter 21mm. Above the window 'Patent 21487/24' which refers to the grooved top-cap. On the mouthpiece 'A.A', Automobile Association. Right; 'M.E.T', Metropolitan Electric Tramways.*

Below: *J Hudson & Co London escargots, standard range medium size, barrel-end diameter 24mm. Left; 'The Harold A Wilson Co Ltd Hawco Toronto', late 1920s. Centre; 'A C Spalding & Bros Ltd Made in Gt Britain Trade Mark Spalding', above the window 'Patent 21487/24', late 1920s. Right; mouthpiece marked 'The Thunderer Hudson's Patent', 1897-1911.*

J Hudson & Co London escargots, standard range, largest size, barrel-end diameter 26mm. Left; mouthpiece marked 'J Hudson & Co Birmingham 1917', black oxydised finish. Back stamped 'Patent'. Goods are usually only marked in this way for the life of the patent, which in this case was 1897-1911. Perhaps a marked obsolete component was used or it was struck in error. Centre; mouthpiece marked 'The Thunderer J Hudson & Co Patent Barr St Birmingham'. Right; Barrel-end marked 'L.P.T.B', London Passenger Transport Board, 1940s. L.P.T.B was nationalised and became the L.T.E, London Transport Executive.

Below: *J Hudson & Co London escargots. Left; inexpensive thin gauge, 'The Thunderer', 1940s, barrel-end diameter 20mm. Centre; small size with long mouthpiece, front top and bottom having lips. Made from the 1960s onwards, common, barrel-end diameter 19mm. Right; standard medium size but with a bottom lip, 1930s, barrel-end diameter 24mm, rare.*

Below: *J Hudson & Co. Bottom lip of the medium sized escargot illustrated left. Model 059½, 1930s. Rare.*

Below: *J Hudson & Co London escargots. Left & centre; both marked on the top of the mouthpiece 'G.C.T', Glasgow Corporation Tramways, and backstamped with the serial numbers 586 & 189. Both have side plates and the centre whistle has a reinforced mouthpiece, late 1920s. Right; this splendid whistle has strengthening side plates and mouthpiece reinforcement of 'D' cross section wire. Marked on the side 'Patent 10898.'08', finger grip loop made to Registered Design 571315, 1910. 'B.C.T', Birmingham Corporation Transport, 1910-1922.*

Left: *J Hudson & Co London escargots. Left; additional side plates to the barrel-ends depicting a dog's head. The dog's head design has been used since the mid 1880s, this example 1920s. Right; strengthening side plates to the sides to prevent wear to the joints., 'S.C.T', Sheffield Corporation Transport, 1920s.*

Right: *J Hudson & Co London escargots. Back left; largest size, tapered mouthpiece, barrel-end marked 'European Football Championship 1996 Final Draw Birmingham 17-12-95'. Normally finished in polished brass, this example gold plated. Back right; largest size with finger grips, no top-cap but body bears a location pressing, late 1920s-30s. Calls with finger grips were available in all sizes. Front left; medium size with built-in German made compass, (fitted to all whistle sizes) no markings on whistle, late 1920s-30s. Front right; medium size, hallmarked silver, side engraved 'Final Cavalry Cup 1937 Referee R.S.M. M. Jones'. All sizes have been made in silver.*

Above: *J Hudson & Co London escargots with tapered mouthpieces. This small whistle was made from 1899, Registered Design 337076. From the 1910s until the late 1930s they were available fitted with a compass in the side and during the 1920s they briefly had sides with a ring design. In the 1960s rubber mouthpiece covers could be supplied. Left; replica RAF air-crew whistle made by Hudsons in the 1990s. One side marked 'A.M. (crown symbol) 23/230', the other blank. Top of the mouthpiece marked 'The Acme Thunderer Made In England' and the top-cap has a groove. Made in plated and unplated brass. Centre left; genuine issued RAF air-crew whistle from the Second World War. One side marked 'A.M. (crown symbol) 23/230', the other 293/14/L1795'. Top of the mouthpiece unmarked and the top-cap has no groove, plated brass, 1940s. Centre right; one side marked 'Patent' the other Rd 337076', a Hudson Registered Design of April 1899. Knop top, 1910s. Right; mouthpiece marked 'Abbey Cyclone', Abbey is the name of a sports company.*

Right: *J Hudson & Co London escargot with a tapering mouthpiece attached to a leather wristlet marked 'Made in England', 1960s, overall length 250mm. Originally a patent of 1907. Various escargots, general service whistles and sirens have all been available attached to either a pigskin or leather wristlet.*

Left: *J Hudson & Co London escargots with tapered mouthpieces. The small size made from 1899, the medium size from the 1930s and the large size from mid 1940s. In the 2000s all three sizes were still produced and all were available with finger grips. Back row; small & large size with finger grips. Front left; 'BMMO', Birmingham & Midland Motor Omnibus Company, modern. Front centre; 'L.P.T.B', London Passenger Transport Board, 1940s. Front right; large size, hallmarked silver, 1992.*

Right: *J Hudson & Co London escargot. Around the largest size escargot is affixed pressings portraying a Great War tank. The fixing necessitated bending over the corners of the pressing around the mouthpiece which gives the appearance that the end of the whistle has suffered a blow. Available in the 1920s and perhaps for some time before that date, 61mm. A rare sought-after whistle.*

METAL GLASGOW ESCARGOTS

The first recognised Glasgow whistle was by S Auld of Glasgow, a Registered Design of 1890, shortly followed by J Hudson & Co's Patent 19868 of 1891. This patent whistle is made from three pieces plus a top fitting. One blank is shaped to form the sides of the barrel and mouthpiece top, another for the barrel and mouthpiece bottom, and the final piece is the tongue.

This escargot was made in three sizes until the 1970s since when only the largest size has been manufactured. It is Hudson's most powerful escargot and in the 2000s the basic elements of the 1890 configuration survives. Various modifications have been made over the years to the design of the top fitting and the tongue, and it is by examining the changes made to these two components that examples may be dated.

Top fitting a knop

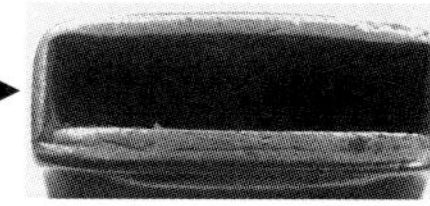

Tongue straight at front. 1890s-1923

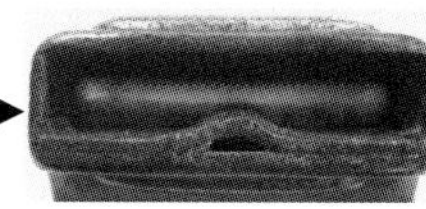

Tongue with inverted 'U' at front. Early 1920s

Top fitting a cap. Patent 214519/1923.

No groove in top of cap. c.1939-40s

Groove in top cap

Top of mouthpiece not marked Made in England

Tongue straight at front. 1923-30s

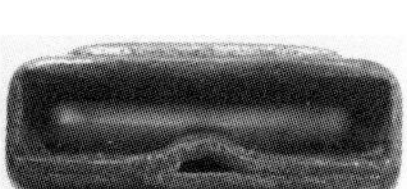

Tongue with inverted 'U' at front. Early 1920s

Top of mouthpiece marked Made in England

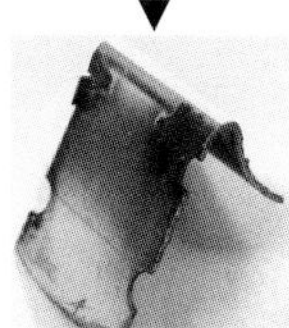

The tongue can be viewed by looking into the front of the whistle. The flat part assists dating. The curved part goes into the barrel.

Tongue plain 1940s-50s

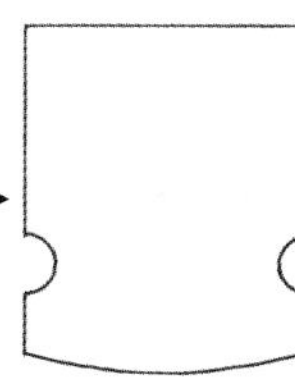

Tongue with semi-circular cutouts at each side near the front 1960s

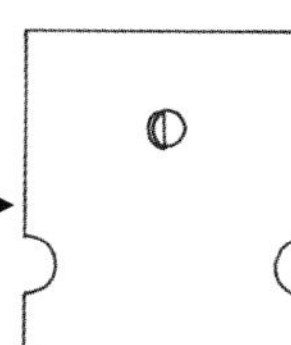

Tongue with semi-circular cutouts at each side near the front plus *a raised pressing centralised at the back. Late 1960s-70s*

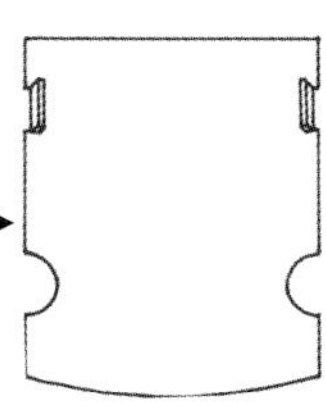

Tongue with semi-circular cutouts at each side near the front plus *a raised pressing at each side at the back. 1970s onwards*

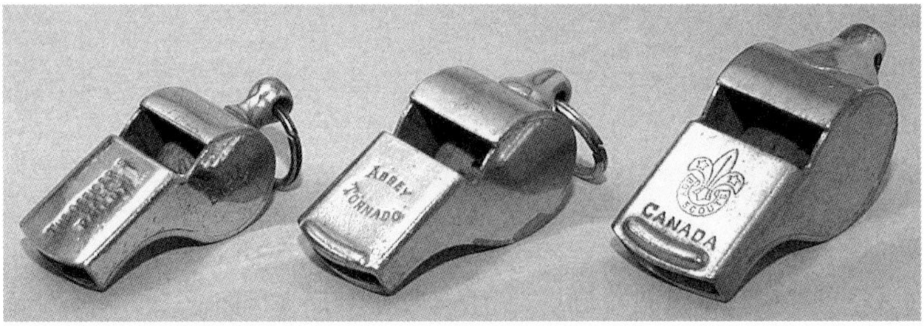

J Hudson & Co Glasgow escargots. Standard sizes, barrel-end diameters 20mm, 23mm & 27mm. Left; 'R McQueen & Sons Newcastle' 'The Thunderer Hudson's Patent', 1900s. Centre; 'Abbey Tornado'. 'Abbey' being the name of a sports company and 'Tornado' the whistle's marketing name. 'Tornado' was later used by Hudson for a range of plastic whistles. Right; Scouting whistle. 'Canada' and fleur-de-lis symbol.

J Hudson & Co's second Glasgow escargot patent was number 12181 of 1906. This escargot was constructed from two blanks plus a top fitting. One blank, as in the first patent, became the sides of the barrel and the top of the mouthpiece. The second blank fashioned everything else, including the tongue. This second blank was in essence a metal strip, the end section of which, when viewed from the side was almost triangular, with two curved sides. The triangular section filled the gap between the bottom of the mouthpiece and the barrel—without it the whistle would resemble a London escargot. No examples of this call are known.

An important design development which can act as a bench-mark in the identification and dating of escargots is a patent cap-like top fitting, number 21387 of 1923, which superseded the almost-spherical knop. During manufacture the cap is held tight to the shoulders of the whistle, prior to soldering, by wire running round the whistle and along the groove in the top of the cap. The size and shape of the cap has changed over the years and with a representative collection of whistles the changes can be clearly seen.

J Hudson & Co largest size Glasgow escargots. Left; silver, hallmarked J H & Co, 1901, engraved crest above the window. Centre; nickel plated brass with finger grips, c.2000. The three standard sizes of escargots are all made with finger grips. Right; the whistle is coated with a cream coloured plastic, and additionally with a purple plastic coating to the front of the mouthpiece and around the top-cap, tongue 'U' shaped, late 1920s. The purpose of the coating is to prevent sticking to the lips in very cold weather.

Above: *J Hudson & Co largest size Glasgow escargots with barrel-ends that have the addition of extra side plates to prevent wear at the joints. Made in three sizes from 1908 until the 1940s when only the largest size was produced until the 1960s. Left; marked above the window 'Patent 213487/24', which pertains to the grooved top-cap which replaced the knop, made in the 1920s. Right; the whistle has in addition to side plates, a wire of 'D' cross section that goes completely around the mouthpiece to facilitate the retention of the whistle in the mouth. Side plate marked 'Patent 10898.'08', which is the patent pertaining to the strengthening measures, 1908-1922. Mouthpiece marked 'B.C.T', Birmingham Corporation Transport.*

Right: *J Hudson & Co from 1899, initially for ten years, and then until the early 1920s, made Glasgow thunderers for McPherson Brothers marked in various ways including, 'The Glasgow Thunderer' 'McPherson Brothers Ltd Argyle St Glasgow', and 'The Thunderer Patent', plus the addresses '78 Argyle St' and '31 Queen St'.*

Below: *J Hudson & Co. 'The Officer's Call'. Made in three sizes, marked No.1, 2, & 3: Size 1, the smallest, is the most difficult to find. Usually marked J Brown & Son, Glasgow. Normally in plated brass but this hard-to-find example in plated zinc, 1930s.*

Below: *J Hudson & Co small size escargot attached to a wristlet, Patent 25619/1907 overall length 240mm. All sizes were obtainable attached to the wristlet, as were sirens and general service whistles. The strap used was generally leather, though pigskin was also used, and examples can be found with the patent number stamped into the wristlet.*

J Hudson & Co Patent 447673 of 1936. Cast in antimonial lead in two interlocking halves held together by two eyelets. Made in one size only, discontinued in the early 1940s. The resin based version is shown in the next section which features plastic escargots.

J Hudson & Co. Left; 'Titanic', a souvenir whistle produced from 1998 onwards when a film of the same name was released. Made in very large numbers, however, the original first issue packaging is a collectors' item. The illustration on the box supplied with the escargot shows a whistle marked 'SS Titanic'. This was incorrect on two counts; the whistle itself is only marked 'Titanic' and the real Titanic was styled 'RMS'. The box was quickly redesigned and the new packaging included a photograph of an actual whistle. Right; 'L.&N.E.R' whistle made in the 1990s for the souvenir and gift trade. It was never used by the L&NER. New whistles with railway company markings, including SR and LMS have also been made. These new whistles are sometimes traded at prices which old whistles realise. It is straightforward to distinguish between new and old calls by referring to the dating chart on page 23.

PLASTIC GLASGOW ESCARGOTS

All Hudson plastic whistles are of the Glasgow type, the nature of the material does not recommend the London shape. In 1926 Hudsons began making compression moulded escargots using Bakelite, and were one of only twelve companies in the country using this material for their products. It was particularly suitable for whistles that were intended for use in sub-zero temperatures as, unlike metal, it did not stick to the skin or lips. Earlier, in 1914 Hudsons had registered the word 'Acmeoid' as a trademark (now obsolete) and used the name to market a range of plastic round pea whistles made in assorted colours. The use of the trademark was extended to include Bakelite Glasgow escargots from 1926 when production in three sizes commenced (it was previously thought that production of this range started in 1914). The word 'Acmeoid' is seen on the underside of the escargots as part of a logo which includes a company monogram and the word, 'England'; from the 1940s 'Acmeoid' no longer appeared instead 'Made in England' was placed on the top of the mouthpiece. In the 2000s the three sizes continue to be made. The largest size has always been obtainable with finger grips. The earliest 'Acmeoid' calls with finger grips were made without the cap-shaped moulding that could take a split ring. This was followed by a period when a shaped cap was present and finally the cap was removed again. Variations of the largest size include those in which the barrel-end has been modified. One diversification had a side where the actual moulding incorporated the initials of a railway company. Another had a metal plate set into the barrel-end, bearing details of a company or organisation.

This was done by placing the metal plate in the barrel-end mould, filling it with Bakelite powder and compressing the two together. Late 20th century patterns have pozigrip sides whose patterned surfaces discourage the fingers from slipping. At the end of the 20th century a composite pattern was made from the smallest size combined with a fixed-pitch dog whistle (see page 72).

Above: *J Hudson & Co plastic escargots. Illustrated are early compression moulded bakelite whistles produced from 1926 until the 1940s. A stylised J H Co monogram is moulded into the back, around the words 'Acemeoid England'. The mouthpiece top is marked 'The Acme Thunderer'. In the late 1940s 'Made In England' was added and the back became plain. Barrel-end diameters, 20mm, 25mm & 28mm.*

J Hudson & Co. Monogram at the back of Bakelite escargots, 1926 to the late 1940s. 'JHCo Acmeoid England'.

Below: *J Hudson & Co. Side plates of plastic escargots. Top left; 'S.R', Southern Railway. Rare when the lettering is moulded into the plastic as this example. 'Acmeoid England' at back. Top right; 'CIA', Central Intelligence Agency, USA, early 1970s. Bottom left; 'L.T.E', London Transport Executive, 1950s. Bottom right; 'BR(S)', British Rail Southern Region, late 1940s.*

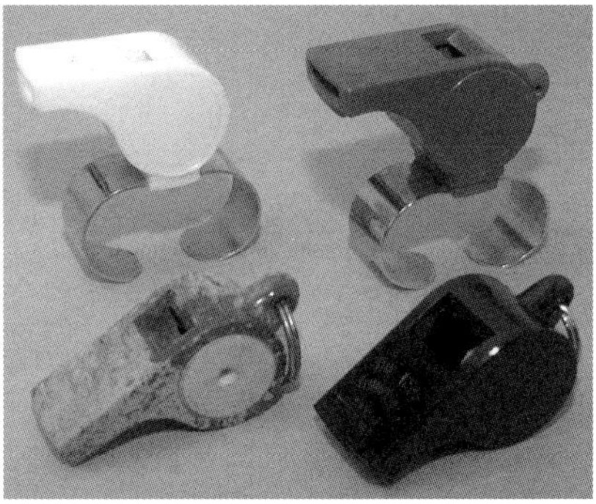

Left: *J Hudson & Co largest size plastic escargots. Back left; white with finger grips, moulding to take a split ring not present, top marked 'The Acme Thunderer', 1926-40s. Back right; maroon with finger grips, top marked 'The Acme Thunderer Made In England', moulding above window to take a split ring present, late 1940s-c.80s. Early examples from this period had the finger grips attached by slotted screws, later by pozidrive screws. Front left; mottled walnut with cream side piece with a stop-hole, 1926-40s. Rare with stop-hole. Front right; modern whistle in black with pozigrip sides, c.2000. It can be supplied with finger grips and, as models from the 1926-40s, when so supplied it has no moulding above the window to take a split ring.*

J Hudson & Co. Plastic escargots, Patent 620720/1945. Top; 'B.R', British Rail. Bottom; 'NRS', National Railway Supplies.

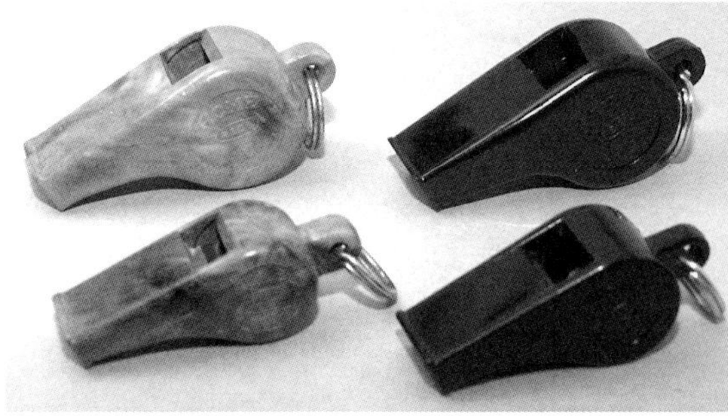

J Hudson & Co plastic escargots. The first three whistles described below were made to Patent 620720, valid from 1949 to 1965, for making plastic whistles in two pieces. Back left; mottled blue-grey, one side marked 'Patent No 620720' in a curved style, length 59mm. The earliest examples were made before the patent was granted and a side was marked 'Patents Pending'. Available in two sizes in a range of colours including black, cream, and mottled in blue, green, pink and red. Back right; one side moulded 'B.R', British Rail. Since the break up of BR in 1994 look out whistles marked 'NRS', National Railway Supplies, have been available. This injection moulded whistle in black is still available in the 2000s for general consumption, one side marked 'Acme Regd Made In England', the other 'Patent No 620720' in a straight style of lettering. Front left; small model, length 50mm, details the same as the large model. Front right; the modern version of the previous whistle marked 'Tested and Guaranteed', now slightly wider and longer, made from the 1970s onwards. Available with finger grips.

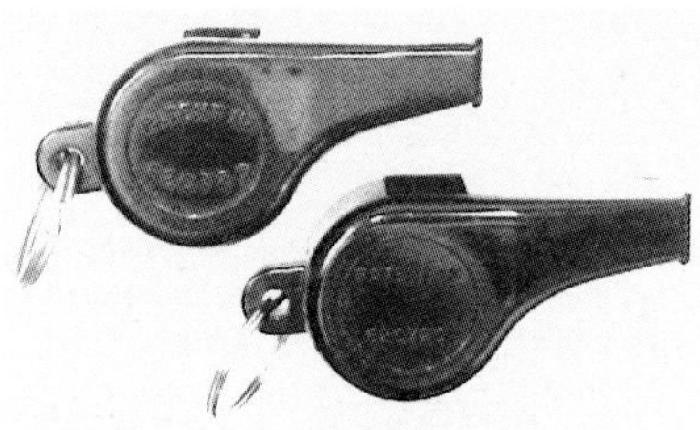

J Hudson & Co. Plastic escargots, Patent 620720. Top; old whistle with patent details curved. Bottom; new whistle with patent details in a straight line.

Above: *J Hudson & Co plastic escargots. Patent 447673/1936. Made in two halves fixed together with eyelets. One side marked with the patent number, made in black and in walnut, lengths 52mm & 62mm. Hudson's production probably ceased when Cascelloid (Palitoy) made the whistle under licence in the late 1940s – see under Cascelloid.*

J Hudson & Co plastic escargots. Left; souvenir whistle made to Patent 447673/1936 for George VI's coronation in 1936. One half in red, the other in black with a red, white and blue lanyard with a button hook, attached by a white enamelled split ring. To the red side is attached a printed depiction of George VI and his consort Queen Elizabeth. Originally a profile of Edward VIII was moulded into the plastic but this was removed after his abdication. Edward VIII examples are known to exist. Right; festive Samba escargot, Model 475, with a yellow body, made from the 1990s. Instead of plain barrel-ends, open conical hollow components in green and red have been fitted which maybe closed with the fingers. This effectively enables several notes to be sounded. Supplied with a yellow, green and red lanyard.

M Y DART CO (GAMES) LTD
This company, located in Barnet, made a number of chrome plated escargots marked with the trademark 'Halex'. They also made whistles marked 'Mitre'. M Y Dart later became M Y Sports & Games Ltd.

In 1973 seven different models, in two sizes were advertised, all London escargots. One large model had a mouthpiece with parallel sides and a further pattern was available with finger grips. The remaining five models all had tapered mouthpieces. Two were medium sized and were made with or without end-caps to the barrel. and the same was true for two large models. The final model was a large size without end-caps but fitted with finger grips.

M Y Dart Co (Games) Ltd. Left; small size with end caps, 'Halex Regd Made In England'. Centre; large size, 'Mitre Made In U.K', barrel-end diameter 25mm. Right; large size with finger grips, 'Halex Regd Made In England'.

P McDONALD
Whistles were constructed using six pieces, similar to Auld's escargots. Only one model of escargot made by Peter McDonald is known, it is possible others exist.

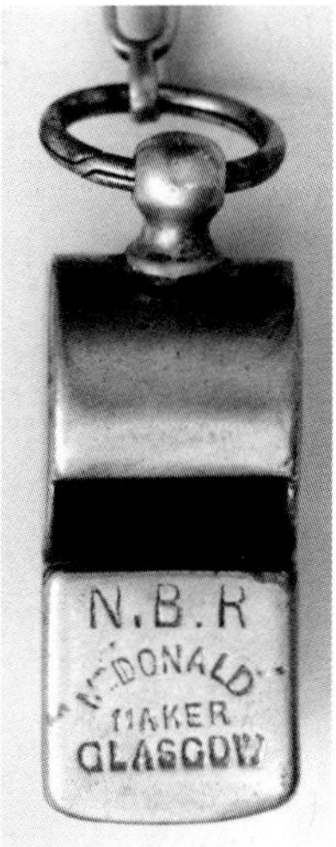

P McDonald escargot. 'N.B.R McDonald Maker Glasgow', North British Railway, 1890, barrel-end diameter 25mm. McDonald applied with H A Ward for a patent in 1890 but it was later abandoned. McDonald calls are probably the rarest of all escargots.

McPHERSON BROTHERS
McPherson Brothers of Glasgow did not manufacture escargots although whistles bearing their name often included the word, 'Makers'. They were ironmongers, cutlers, hardware vendors and stockists of gun and fishing tackle. Whistles were supplied to them by Black & Co and later by J Hudson & Co under whose names the details and illustrations of their whistles can be found.

PALITOY
See under Cascelloid Ltd.

R PRINGLE & SONS

Robert Pringle & Sons of Wilderness Works, Middlesex was a London company of silversmiths, refiners and jewellers dating from the 19th century until 1968.

R Pringle & Sons, London escargot. Silver plated nickel silver with the original cylindrical 'pea', top fitting a winged 'V'. Also made in unplated nickel silver, 1950s-60s. Barrel-end diameter 26mm.

R Pringle & Sons, London escargot. Trademark backstamp, crossed axes and the letters 'WW' (Wilderness Works) within a circle.

RUDD BROS

Rudd Bros of Abbey Street, Birmingham, made a range of extremely inexpensive whistles.

Rudd Bros. Tin plate London escargots intended for the toy and festive cracker market, 1920s-30s. Length of largest 44mm.

R A WALTON

R A Walton manufactured three patterns and gave each a name. His Glasgow whistle was marked 'The Roller' but no examples of this whistle have been seen. He made two London escargots; 'The Rattler' with a tapering mouthpiece, and the 'Rouser' with a parallel sided mouthpiece and a top fitting looking almost as though it had been made with wire. The 'Rouser' was similar in style to those made by C T Willet.

R A Walton London escargot. Top of mouthpiece marked 'The Rattler', nickel plated brass, c.1900. Barrel-end diameter 21mm. Rare.

H A WARD

Whistles made by Arthur Ward of Glasgow are probably the rarest of all escargots after those made by Peter McDonald. His pattern was constructed from six pieces in a way similar to Auld's design. With Peter McDonald of Birmingham he applied for a patent, later abandoned, which appears in the records as number 2980, 25 February 1890. This was less than a month after Auld's registered design was lodged. Two sizes of Glasgow escargot are known, models No.23 & No.24.

Left: *H A Ward, Glasgow escargot, Model No.24, 'Alpha Improved Call No.24', backstamped 'Patent No 2980'. Side plate 'L.M.S', London Midland & Scottish Railway, 1890, barrel-end diameter 22mm. Very rare.*

Right: *H A Ward, Glasgow escargot, Model No.23. 'Alpha Improved Call No23'. Backstamped 'H.A.W Bm Pl Patent'. 'Bm' for Birmingham and 'Pl' for Provisional. Nickel plated brass, 1890, barrel-end diameter 25mm. Rare.*

C T WILLETS

C T Willets, Birmingham, produced a small London escargot. The whistle is formed from four pieces; a top fitting, two end-caps and an 'L' shaped brass strip. On arm of the 'L' is curved round to form the barrel of the whistle and the bottom of the mouthpiece. The other is folded over three times and soldered to complete the mouthpiece.

The whistle's mouthpiece design is similar to one used by A De Courcy & Co but was not one employed by J Hudson & Co. However, Willets did have made by Hudsons a general service whistle marked 'C.T.W'.

Left: *C T Willet, Birmingham. London escargot. 'C.T.W's Rouser', no tooth-grips. Nickel plated brass with a hollow spherical knop with a small diameter hole, diameter 21mm, 1920s-30s.*

Right: *C T Willet London escargot. Alternative type of top loop; a wire of 'D' cross section.*

Beaufort whistles

Beaufort whistles have the appearance of a tapered tube, the narrowest end being placed in the mouth. In the 1860s they were recognised as railway whistles and then as police whistles. Light infantry regiments use silver and silver plated patterns attached to chains. and supplied with a case which is fastened to the cross belt of officers' uniforms.

Perhaps it was fashion, or the fact that the police began to be issued with Beaufort whistles, that led to railway companies changing to calls with a 'pea' - either a round pea whistle or an escargot.

The Beaufort whistle was abandoned by most police forces, for example, Lancashire, Birmingham, Salford, Lincolnshire and Bradford, with the rise in popularity of the general service whistle (the Bobby's whistle) in the mid 1880s. J Hudson & Co, the main supplier, offered to take back Beaufort whistles but one notable exception, Liverpool City Police, retained it for some years before changing to the general service whistle. This is the probable explanation as to why Beaufort whistles issued to police forces are difficult to find with the exception of those to Liverpool City Police.

It is difficult to decide who the makers were of many Beaufort whistles, but where possible distinguishing details are given. Dating of most, to within a few years, is almost impossible as each maker's design and construction remained the same throughout the period of manufacture.

J Barrall, 1886-98. Beaufort whistles. Left; 'Liverpool City Police Warranted Perfect Barrall Birmingham', length 77mm. Right; 'Birmingham Police Warranted Perfect Barrall Birmingham'. Both rare.

J Barrall, 1886-98. Beaufort whistles with mouthpieces, probably made by J Barrall. Centre whistle marked 'City Police', length 75mm.

A De Courcy & Co, 1888-1927. The 'Assistance' with semi-circular windows. Early 20th century.

A De Courcy & Co, 1888-1927. Some models are made with the window nearer to the mouthpiece than J Hudson & Co's Beauforts. Largest whistle 85mm, nickel plated brass, 1910s to late 1920s. Right whistle marked 'Liverpool City Police'.

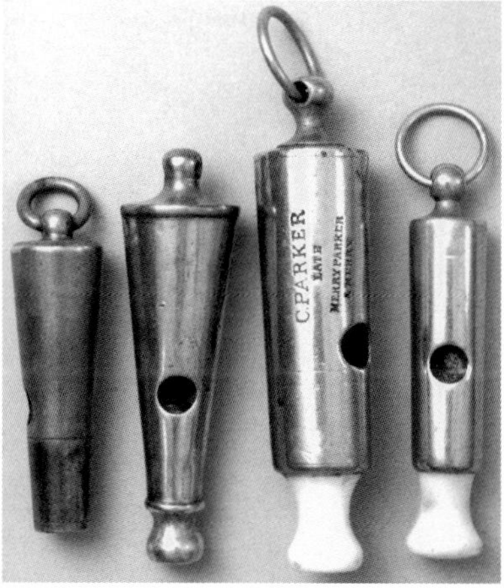

J Dixon & Sons Beaufort whistles, 19th century. Left; unmarked, length 58mm. Centre left; unmarked nickel plated brass. Centre right; 'C Parker Late Merry Parker & Merry', ivory mouthpiece, nickel silver, rare. Right; unmarked with ivory mouthpiece, nickel silver, rare.

Below: *W Dowler & Sons Beaufort whistles, 19th to early 20th century. Left; 'Hiatt', makers of police equipment, solid knop, not hollow, length 73mm. Centre left; 'Maidstone Police Dowler & Sons 94 Gt Charles St Birmingham', solid knop. Centre right; the whistle is combined with an escargot, Kent Constabulary button end-caps. The barrel is marked 'Hiatts' Constabulary Whistle No 225730', a Registered Design of 1894, rare. Right; rare in having a circular wire tooth-grip, 'W.C.C', Worcester County Council, at the back in an oval 'W Dowler Birmm'.*

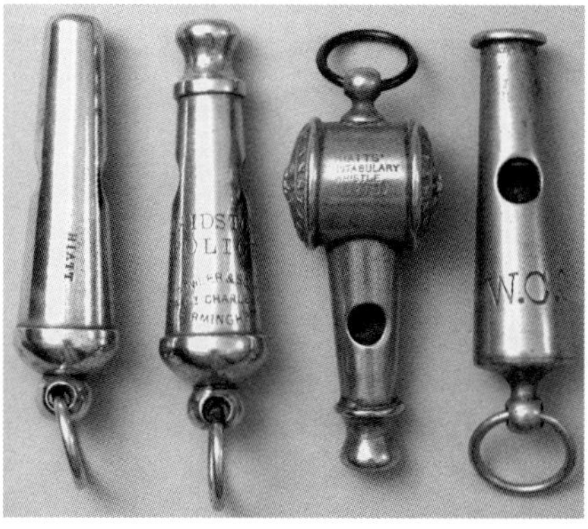

J Dixon & Sons high quality Beaufort whistles, late 19th to early 20th century. Left to right; unmarked, length 69mm; 'Merry Phipson & Parker', top loop a circular wire; 'Dixon & Sons', nickel silver, very high quality; unmarked nickel silver, very high quality'; 'Preist Oxford St'; 'Dixon & Sons', very high quality.

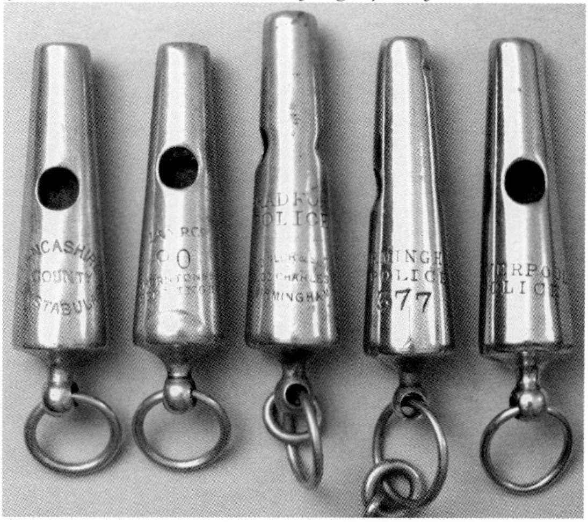

Above: *W Dowler & Sons Beaufort whistles, 19th to early 20th century. Dowler's Beaufort whistles can generally be identified by the shape of the diaphragm, which is a wedge more truncated than those by J Hudson & Co – when viewed up the mouthpiece the widish flat end of the wedge can be seen. Left; 'Lancashire County Constabulary', length 70mm. Centre left; 'L & YRCo 90 Thornton & Son Birmingham', Lancashire & Yorkshire Railway, '90' is the railway company's serial number. Centre; 'Bradford Police Dowler & Sons 94 Gt Charles St Birmingham'. Centre right; 'Birmingham Police 377'. Right; 'Liverpool Police', at the back in an oval 'W Dowler Birmm'.*

J R GAUNT & SON

Patent 22309 of 1911 describes a Beaufort whistle made from two sheet metal pressings soldered together. No examples are known.

J HUDSON & CO

The diaphragms used by Hudsons for Beaufort whistles were shaped as a wedge or as a flat disc with tines (finger-like projections) pointing either towards, or away from, the mouthpiece. Beaufort whistles were also combined with one or more additional whistles so as to provide a single instrument with enhanced signalling capabilities. Production of Beauforts ceasd in the 1950s, with the exception of the 3-in-one shepherd's whistle, see page 71, which was available up to the 1970s.

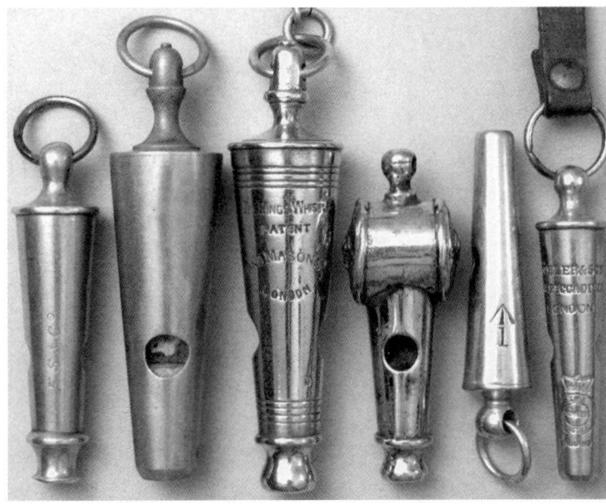

Right: *J Hudson & Co Beaufort whistles. Left to right; engraved 'F.S & Co', nickel silver, 1920s, length 76mm; large unmarked call; 'The King's Whistle Patent Shand Mason & Co London', length 99mm, very rare. The 'Patent' refers to Hudson first patent, a diaphragm design of 1885, number 435. Shand Mason were a company supplying fire-fighting equipment. The King's Whistle is probably one of Hudson's finest whistles; Beaufort whistle combined with an escargot, the barrel-ends made from Devon Constabulary tunic buttons, rare. Made to Hiatts Registered Design probably after the registration was no longer valid; body marked '↑1', indicating it was issued to troops in British India; call complete with leather strap. Marked above the window 'Köhler & Son 185 Piccadilly London' and below in a circle, a crown with 'The Köhler Whistle England'.*

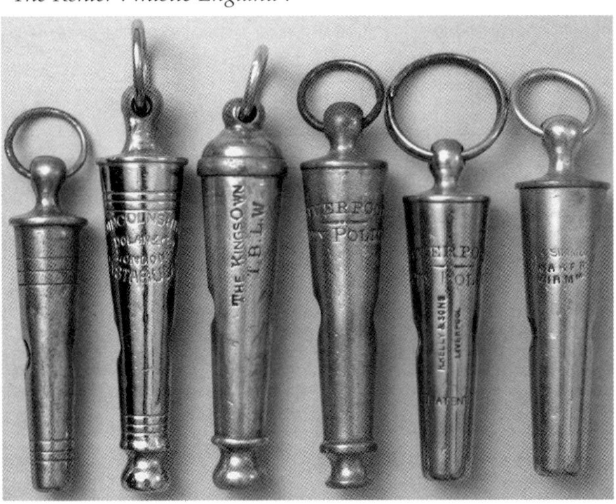

Left: *J Hudson & Co Beaufort whistles. Left to right; call with rings around the body, 1930s, length 71mm; 'Lincolnshire Constabulary Dolan & Co London'. Dolans were the company through whom the whistle was ordered; 'The King's Own' with the unidentified initials 'T.B.L.W'. This whistle was advertised in the 1900s as 'The Cyclists Own', hollow top knop; 'Liverpool City Police', with mouthpiece; 'Liverpool City Police R Kelly & Sons Liverpool Patent'. Kelly were the company through whom the whistle was ordered, and 'Patent' refers to Hudsons patent diaphragm of 1898, valid until 1912; 'Jas Simmons Maker Birmm'.*

Left: *B Lilly & Sons short Beaufort whistle, 'Officer', oval window, 1900s, length 59mm, rare.*

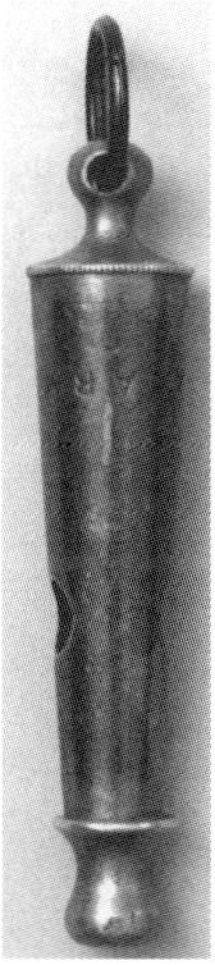

Right: *B Lilly & Sons nickel plated brass Beaufort whistle, 'Alarm', 1900s, length 83mm*

Above left: *Smith & Wright Beaufort whistle, 'Liverpool Police Smith & Wright Ltd Birmingham', late 19th early 20th century, nickel silver, length 72mm. The whistle was probably ordered through Smith & Wright but made by W Dowler & Sons. The diaphragm is Dowler's truncated wedge design.*

Above: *Thomas Yates Beaufort whistles, late 19th century. Illustrated are whistles in addition to those shown in Yates' catalogue of 1870 reproduced on pages 49 and 50. Left; 'N.E.R T.Yates', North Eastern Railway, nickel silver, length 76mm. Centre left; nickel silver. Centre right; Britannia metal. Right; crown metal.*

Smith & Wright Beaufort whistles of the 1890s made from light gauge brass. Left; top-cap marked 'Rd No 191579', a Registered Design of 1892, length 53mm.

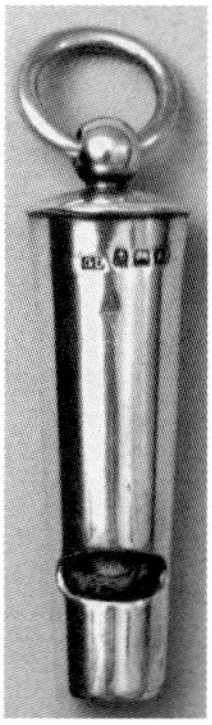

George Unite silver Beaufort whistle, hallmarks for Birmingham, 1925, length 62mm.

Left: *Military infantry Beaufort whistles. The whistles had their own cases that attached to the crossbelt which went across the chest together with a triple length of chain that terminated in a circular plate embossed with a lion's head or regimental motif. Left; made by Bent & Parker, hallmarked 1863, length in case, as shown, 87mm. Centre; the top of the whistle made like a turret, embossed 'Ubique', the motto of the Royal Artillery. Right; made by Jennens & Co, hallmarked 1899, three chains attached to the top of the whistle ending in a lion's head attached to a plate marked 'Rifle Brigade'.*

Round whistles

The phrase 'round whistles' has been chosen to describe those calls which are not general service whistles (GSW) but which are round or have a short tube-like appearance. The majority contain a pea but those with a stop-hole do not. Some can look similar to a GSW but upon examination will be found to have only one widow. The round whistle may have a mouthpiece like a GSW, or more commonly it is fitted with a fipple similar to some musical instruments, such as the recorder and flageolet. The fipple is a wedge-like piece which forms the back of the mouthpiece and accurately directs the air flow 'uphill' towards the window's edge. This feature can be seen by looking up the mouthpiece. The fipple can be made from a single solid piece or assembled from more than one component. Its design is an important diagnostic feature for determining makers.

Round whistles have been made in a large number of different materials including; gold, silver, nickel silver, brass, Britannia metal and other pewter-related alloys, casting metal, ivory, horn, wood, thermoplastic and thermosetting plastics, and a variety of minerals. Factory volume production has dictated chiefly the use of nickel silver, brass and pewter-like alloys, but in a previous age of now almost-forgotten wage structures and availability of materials, the widespread turning of horn and ivory was practised.

Many round whistles were nickel plated and dealers in collectables frequently remove it, particularly from those examples whose plating is worn in patches. If it is suspected that a call was originally plated verification can often be found by examining inside the mouthpiece and at the base of the top fitting as these are likely places where vestiges of plating may remain.

Making round calls does not necessarily require any special technology or expensive equipment, which has encouraged many silversmiths to produce patterns of their own. Such makers can be traced through the sponsor's mark which is found on sterling silver items.

E Pelletreau of Paris was a wholesale trader who travelled Europe in the 1910s and 1920s, buying and selling whistles made by manufacturers in several countries, notably Britain, Germany and France. J Hudson & Co would buy non-British calls from him and sell them on.

Before the escargot whistle completely took over as the design favoured by railway companies, the round pea whistle, in addition to Beaufort whistles, had been used. They were also kept in stock by the police for use in special situations from about the 1820s—these calls did not have police markings. Round pea whistles were also used by sports people. Only occasionally are round whistles marked with any maker's, seller's or organisation's details.

There has been a huge number of assorted patterns made by manufacturers over many years. The majority of whistles collectors discover will date from the mid nineteenth century to the first half of the twentieth century. Some manufacturers listed in trade directories have left no trace of their patterns. This has led to a number of calls which at present defy identification or dating. This not only applies to whistles made of various pewter-like alloys but also to examples in brass, nickel silver (German silver) and horn. Some manufacturers would impress the body with their name or some other mark, but often they were inconsistent in doing so, for example J Dixon and T Yates. However, in a number of cases unmarked whistles can be identified through having knowledge of similar examples that are marked.

Manufacturers have been identified for as many patterns as possible. Through examining a large number of round whistles it becomes apparent which features are indicative of a particular maker, and which are unreliable—manufacturers tended to imitate each other's patterns.

The following distinctions between whistle designs assist in determining the maker.

(a) Whistles made from a sheet metal blank formed into a tube have a seam where the meeting edges are soldered. Most companies ensured that the seam was always centralised at the back but the following companies did not; J Barrall, Coney & Co, J Dixon & Sons, and T Yates. There are probably a few whistles made by these companies where the seam *is* opposite the window but this would be by chance and not by design.

(b) Some of Dixon's round whistles have a diaphragm which follows the curve of the body *plus* a 'pip' at the circumference, in the centre, see page 40. This 'pip' has been used by Hudson & De Courcy but round whistles with this feature are almost unheard of from these two companies (the 'pip' is a feature of all Hudson general service whistles from 1939).

(c) Stevens & Sons made most round whistles with a diaphragm that gave the appearance of having been cut across three times, see page 47.

(d) The best and quickest way to ascertain whether or not a whistle was made by J Hudson & Co is through their Patent 553 of 1909 which specifies that the plate at the back of the mouthpiece interlocks at three points, see page 43. From this date it was used on all whistles with a fipple; the back of the mouthpiece was marked 'Patent' until the patent expired in 1923. Some whistles before this date can be problematical and care needs to be taken in establishing the identity, as some are similar to those made by De Courcy, T Yates and probably R A Walton.

Several small features when put together, but not reliable by themselves, can lead to an identification. Here would be included the diameter of the body and the distance of the window from the mouthpiece or the top. De Courcy, Hudson and Dixon all produce models with a notched widow but it was *only* in some of Dixon's notched patterns that the corners of the window swept upwards towards the top, see page 40. Windows generally can help in judging age: The oldest calls had rectangular windows with or without a notch, or almost semi-circular ones. By the late 1910s these styles had typically been superseded by one in which the top and bottom of the window were parallel to each other, and the sides were curved.

Caution is needed if evaluating a whistle's provenance from the style of the top. Early tops were made from a casting or solid rod machined to shape. Often there is a 'pip' at the top, to imitate those at the top of horn whistles, which was an addition placed there to hide the hollow left by a lathe's spindle after turning. Later cast tops dispensed with the 'pip'. The cast top was superseded by one made from a sheet metal blank pressed into shape with a separate knop or pillar attached in a rivet-like way. Most round whistles contain a 'pea' (cork ball) but those with a stop-hole do not. A stop-hole is an opening in the body, usually near the top over which a finger may be placed to produce a second note. Rather in the same way as fingers are placed over the holes of woodwind musical instruments.

Note: Many of the whistles illustrated were available in several sizes.

S AULD

Samuel Auld's calls from the 1880s were machined out of solid brass rod or more rarely nickel silver. Two sizes have been noted both with wooden fipples. The larger size has a two-hole fipple, and this pattern of whistle is their well known 'Glasgow Police Call'. In 1907 Aulds, trading from 54 Cowcaddens, Glasgow, sold their whistle business to Hudsons which included the remainder of their stock. Hudsons continued to make Aulds largest size until the 1920s. Auld's original calls may be identified by the milled ring below the almost spherical knop. Often the milling is very worn but a trace can usually be found somewhere. Hudson's productions have no milling around the top and often there is a short pillar instead of a knop.

Auld round whistles made from solid rod, late nineteenth century. The shape of the window provides a convenient way of classifying some whistles as 'Auld-type' where the maker is not known. Left; nickel silver, length 65mm. Centre left; marked down the mouthpiece 'S Auld Maker Glasgow', brass. Centre right; brass, length 57mm. Right; marked down the mouthpiece 'J McFarlane Glasgow'.

Round whistles believed to have been made by S Auld from solid rod, late nineteenth century. Left; brass, length 55mm. Centre; marked down the mouthpiece 'J Christie Maker Glasgow', brass. Right; marked down the mouthpiece 'Reid Gl???', brass.

J BARRALL

Few Barrall whistles are known and those that are have a distinctive shape.

J Barrall slightly tapered nickel silver round whistle with oval window. This example unmarked, though some examples are. A distinctively shaped whistle, mid 1880s-90s, length 56mm. Rare.

Below: *Coney & Co round whistles, distinctive mouthpieces, nickel plated brass, 1900s. Left; the shape of the top is a distinctive Coney shape, length 79mm.*

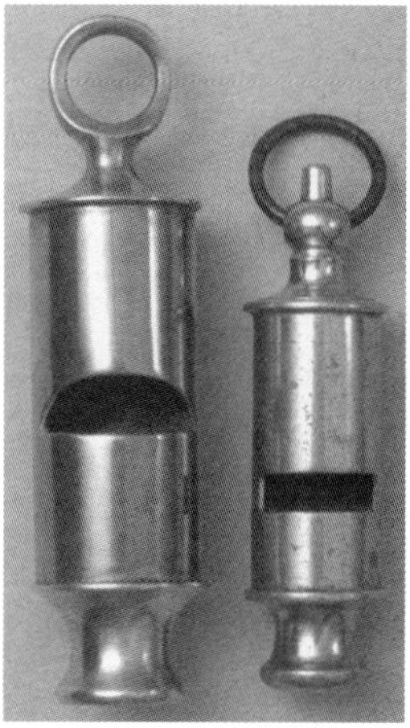

A DE COURCY & CO

Some models are very similar to those made by J Hudson & Co.

Left: *A De Courcy & Co round whistle 1900-1920s, plated brass, length 61mm.*

Above: *A De Courcy & Co round whistles 1888-1927. Left; plated brass, length 59mm. Centre; nickel silver, Auld-type with two-hole fipple, distinguished from Auld and Hudson by the shape of the top. Right; nickel silver.*

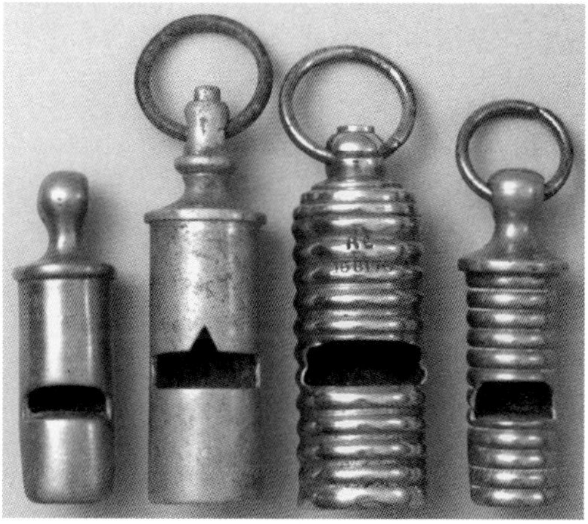

Right: *A De Courcy & Co round whistles. Left; brass, length 44mm. Centre left; nickel silver with notched window. Centre right & right; made to Registered Design 158176/1890. Rare.*

J DIXON & SONS

High quality whistles made in nickel silver, Britannia metal, horn, bone and ivory from the 1880s to the 1930s. Many have a wooden fipple which is made of either ebony or cocoa wood. Frequently whistles are marked with 'Dixon & Sons' and/or with their trumpet and banner trademark. Dixon horn whistles have near semicircular windows. They do not have toothgrips, nor 'acorn' finials as seen on Hudson whistles, however, at times determining whether a whistle was made by Dixons or Hudsons can be inconclusive.

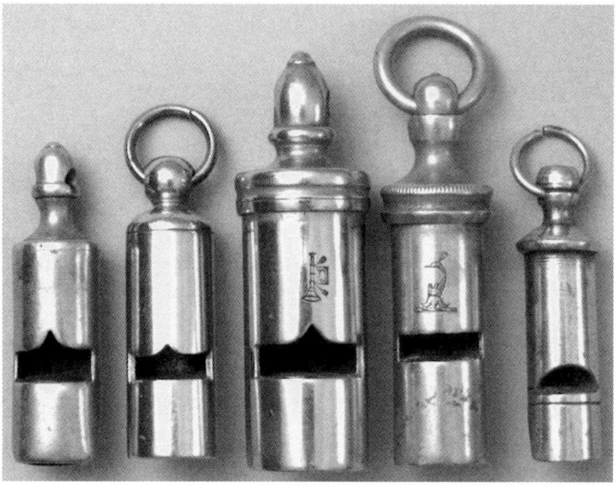

J Dixon & Sons nickel silver whistles. Fourth from the left engraved with a crest above the window. Lengths left to right: 45mm, 42mm, 53mm, 54mm, 41mm.

IDENTIFYING FEATURES OF J DIXON & SONS ROUND WHISTLES

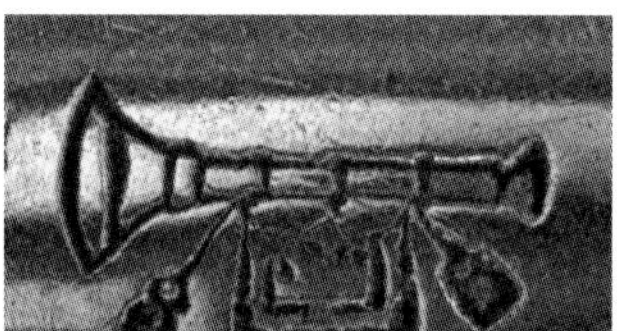

Above: *Trumpet and banner trademark, registered in 1881.*

Right: *View of the diaphragm through the window showing a 'pip' at the circumference.*

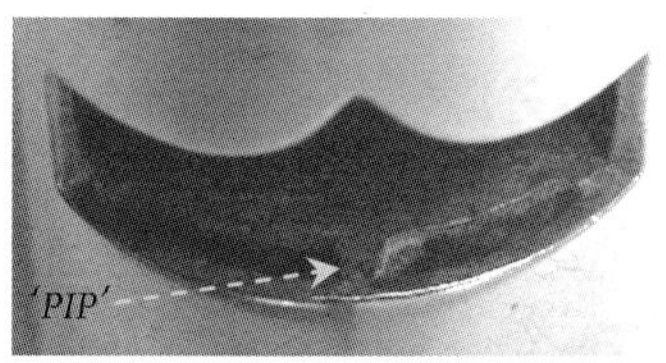

Right: *Squared off top to the knop.*

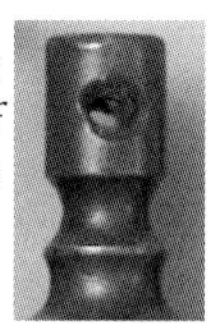

Below: *Whistles made in Britannia metal with a fipple made from cocoa wood that is flat and not curved which is a positive indicator of a Dixon whistle.*

Left: *Several manufacturers made whistles with rectangular windows, with or without notches, but it was only Dixons who also gave them corners that swept upwards.*

Left: *J Dixon & Sons. Left & centre left; nickel silver with a two-hole wooden fipple, lengths 57mm & 63mm. Centre right; nickel silver with stop-hole, length 59mm. Right plated brass, fipple with 'pip' at centre, length 61mm.*

Above: *J Dixon & Sons plated Britannia metal with stop-hole, length 58mm.*

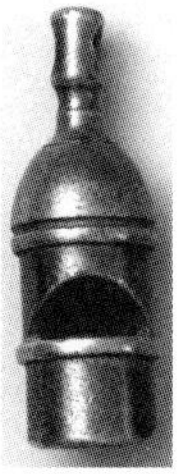

Above: *J Dixon & Sons Britannia metal whistles. All have a wooden fipple as illustrated on the previous page. Length of longest 70mm.*

Above: *J Dixon & Sons Britannia metal whistle with a wooden fipple as illustrated on the previous page. Top of the mouthpiece impressed 'Sykes', the famous powder-flask manufacturers. Almost certainly made by Dixons, length 47mm.*

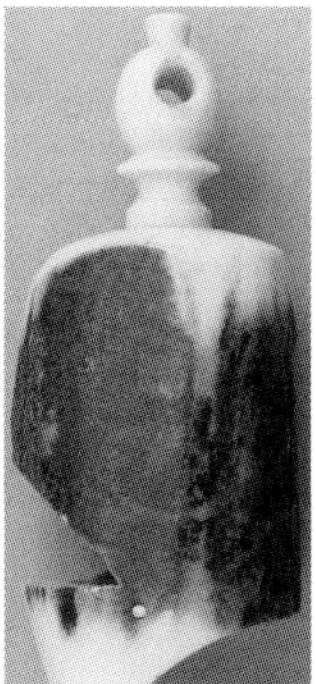

Above: J Dixon & Sons large antler whistle. Maximum diameter 26mm.

Below: *J Dixon & Sons Britannia metal whistles, some nickel plated (pewter will not plate but Britannia metal will). Most have a wooden fipple as illustrated on the previous page. The three calls on the right have squared off tops to the knops – a Dixon feature. Length of longest 63mm.*

Right: *J Dixon & Sons ivory, bone & horn whistles with wooden fipples. Left; eight-sided bone, length 55mm. Centre left; ivory turned to the highest standard – only 1mm thick at the mouthpiece edge. Centre; bone. Centre right; ivory. Right; horn, rectangular with box wood fipple.*

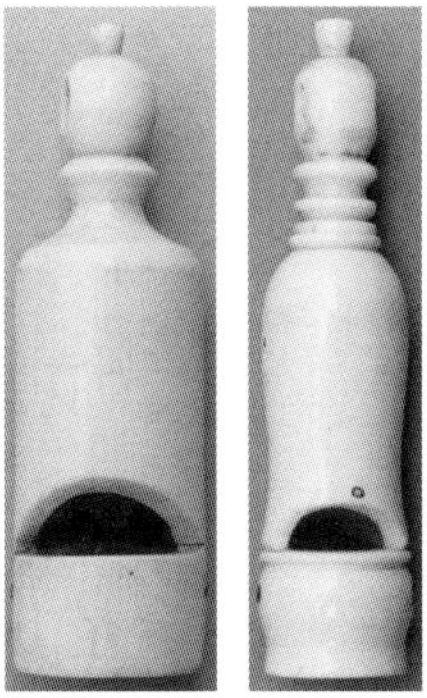

Left: *J Dixon & Sons ivory calls with wooden fipples. Right; distinctive Dixon body shape, length 55mm.*

Left: *J Dixon & Sons large horn whistle, length 85mm. Made in various sizes in this style.*

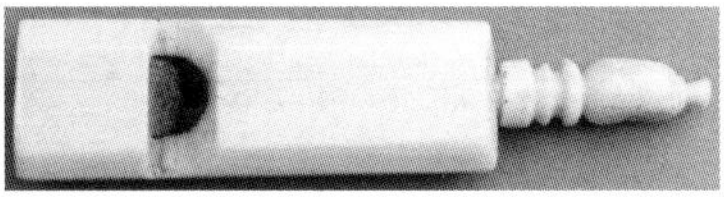

J Dixon & Sons rectangular bone call, length 55mm.

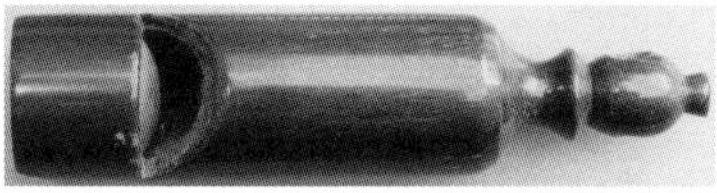

J Dixon & Sons small horn whistle, length 62mm.

W DOWLER & SONS

It is thought that Dowlers did not make round pea whistles. Nevertheless there is a composite whistle, see page 69, consisting of a general service whistle and a round whistle. Probably the round whistle was made by another manufacturer, possible A De Courcy & Co with whom there is inferential evidence that Dowlers had some agreement.

HILL BROS

Only one model is known for Hill Bros, Sheffield, as illustrated.

Hill Bros, horn round pea whistle with finger-ring. Reverse branded 'Rd 220935 G.W.R.', Great Western Railway. The Registered Design dates from November 1893, overall length 83mm. Rare.

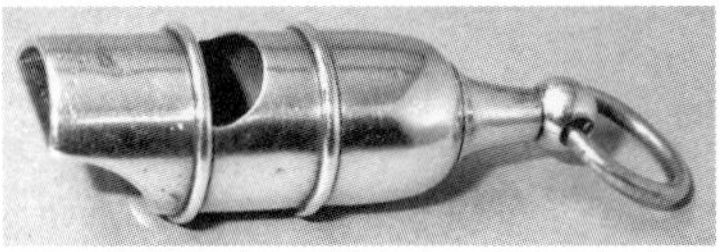

HILLYARD & THOMASON

Hillyard & Thomason round whistle, rubbed silver hallmarks, late nineteenth century, length 59mm.

J HUDSON & CO

From 1909 onwards the plate at the back of the mouthpiece interlocks at three points with the body. This was a feature of Patent 553/1909 and it was used on all appropriately shaped whistles. Until the patent expired in 1923, the back of the mouthpiece was marked 'Patent'. This component is the best way to ascertain whether or not a whistle was made by Hudsons. Some whistles before this date can be problematical and care needs to be taken in establishing the identity as patterns can be very similar to those made by De Courcy, T Yates and R A Walton. Hudsons made a number of patterns which were not standard production models but rather examples of the whistle makers art—most are imitative of patterns made by other manufacturers such as Dowler, Dixon and Yates.

Many Hudson horn whistles have toothgrips and/or 'acorn' finials, features not found on Dixon whistles. The window is often an elongated curve but some are near to being semi-circular. The latter style makes separating some Hudson calls from those by Dixons inconclusive.

Above: *J Hudson & Co mouthpiece back plates. Before Patent 553 of 1909 was granted Hudsons made their mouthpiece back plates in a way similar to other manufacturers—by soldering an appropriately shaped pressing into place (left). Patent 553 specified a back plate that located into the whistle at three points. The plate was marked 'Patent' during its valid period, 1909-23, (centre). After the patent expired the plate was unmarked, (right). The interlocking back plate is a reliable means of identifying Hudson whistles.*

Below: *J Hudson & Co early 20th century horn round whistles with railway company initials branded into the bodies. Left to right: 'Met Rly', Metropolitan Railway, length 71mm; 'S.R', Southern Railway; 'NSR', North Staffordshire Railway; 'L & N.E.R', London & North Eastern Railway; 'GWR', Great Western Railway.*

J Hudson & Co round whistles. Left to right: oval horn, early 20th century, length 58mm; horn, early 20th century; 'The Salvation Army' crest inset into a red Bakelite call, 1930s-40s; Bakelite, 1910s, rare; Bakelite with Bakelite fipple marked 'England', late 1940s-50s; mottled thermoplastic, 1960s.

J Hudson & Co silver round whistles. Most sizes of round whistles were at one time or another made in silver. Those illustrated all have the 'J.H & Co' sponsor's mark, and with the exception of the largest whistle, length 62mm, the Birmingham assay mark (an anchor), and a date letter. Left to right; 1912, 1905, missing, 1926

J Hudson & Co round whistles. The three whistles from the left are all late nineteenth to early twentieth century, made in silver plated nickel silver, nickel silver with toothgrip and nickel plated brass. The call on the right is nickel plated brass and has an unmarked interlocking mouthpiece plate, late 1920s-30s, length 60mm.

J Hudson & Co round whistles. Left to right: mouthpiece plate marked 'Patent', 1909-23, length 44mm; fully engraved body with 'Engeberg 1914'. Given by the Hudson family to acquaintances whilst on holiday, silver plated nickel silver; mouthpiece plate marked 'England', stop-hole, c.1930s; mouthpiece plate not interlocking, pre-1909; 'The Acme Made in England', late 1940s-50s.

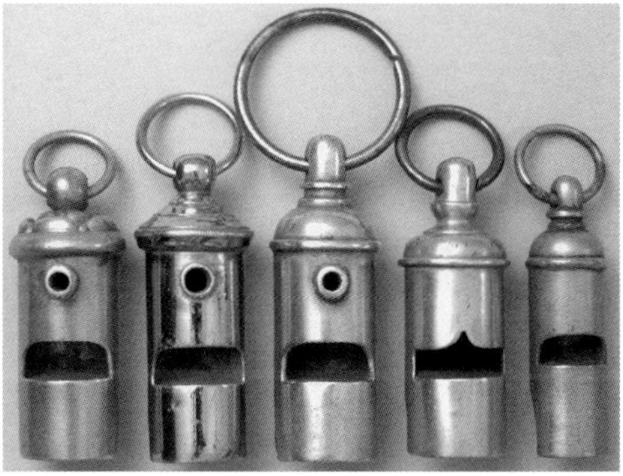

J Hudson & Co round whistles. Left to right: military with a stop-hole, the top-cap with a rose design, 1909-23, length 57mm; military with a stop-hole, the top-cap with concentric rings, chrome plated, c.1900s; body with stop-hole, late 1920s-30s; notched window, late nineteenth to early twentieth century; 1909-23.

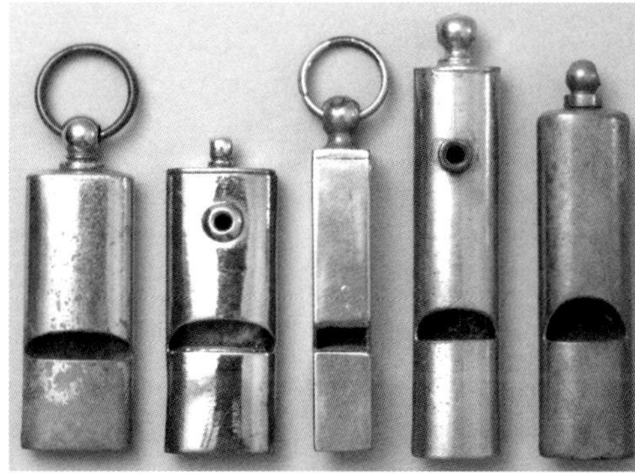

J Hudson & Co fancy small whistles. Left to right: flat oval call marked at the back 'Policia De La Capital' 1900s, length 52mm; flat oval call with stop-hole 1909-23; whistle of square cross section ; oval with stop-hole, 1930s-40s; oval, 1900s.

Above: *J Hudson & Co round whistles. Left to right: 'The Acme Registered Hudson's Patent', made to Patent 435/1885, hollow top knop, 1890s, width 22mm, length 74mm; 'The Acme Registered Patent No 435', the shape of the mouthpiece indicates it was made by James Hudson, 1886-89; the same pattern of whistle, 1908-22; the same pattern of whistle, mid 1920s-30s.*

Below: *J Hudson & Co round whistle. Marked 'S Auld Maker Glasgow', but made by Hudson. Auld sold to Hudsons their whistle making interests and stock in 1907. Hudsons sold off the stock and then made their own whistles which differ in two main respects from Auld's. Firstly, the top has a typical Hudson pillar, not a spherical knop. Secondly, there is no milling below the pillar or to the two 'rings' around the body.*

J Hudson & Co. Shape of the mouthpieces personally made by James Hudson (died 1889), co-founder of Hudsons. Whistles with this feature are rare.

J Hudson & Co round whistles 1890s-1900s. Left to right: the first two are for railway, military or general use. The third call is marked 'L.(?)C.A.B', length 74mm.

Below: *J Hudson & Co round whistles. Left to right: 'The Acme Patent' - diaphragm made to Patent 435/1885, valid 1885-99, length 64mm; 'The Acme Regd' with a brass tag stamped '045', 1910s-20s. Hudson's commercial travellers were given a set of sample whistles to show prospective wholesale buyers, each with a brass tag of the shape illustrated, giving the pattern number; marked 'Redge', steel body with brass top and mouthpiece. Pressed top with ring, 1930s-40s.*

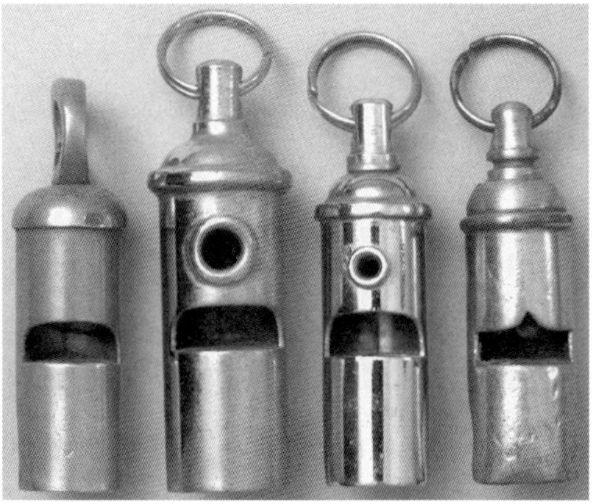

Above: *J Hudson & Co round whistles. Left to right: 1909, 59mm; late 1930s-60s; late 1930s-6s; 1900s.*

Right: *J Hudson & Co round whistles. Left to right: 1930s-40s, length 59mm; back marked 'Policia De La Capital Republica Argentina' around a crest, issued to the Argentinian police, 1900s; unusual whistle in having a circular mouthpiece, 1930s; 1930s.*

J LINEGAR

There are very few whistles which are known for certain to have been make by J Linegar.

J Linegar round whistles. Left; brass with two-hole wooden fipple, length 68mm. Centre; brass with two-hole brass fipple. Right; oval whistle in nickel silver. 1880s. All rare.

J Linegar. Round whistles marked in a curve 'J Linegar' between a star and a crown.

RUDD BROS

Rudd Bros made very inexpensive whistles and it can been seen from their construction that they are little more than tin plate which has been folded into shape. Some German whistles are very similar. They sold their products to the toy trade, to musical instrument retailers and to J Hudson & Co for resale in the 1930s.

Rudd Bros inexpensive tin plate round whistles, 1930s, longest 73mm.

STEVENS & SONS

Stevens & Sons made a number of calls some marked with their name others not. The calls were marked via an overlabel attached to the back of the call. Frequently the body was also marked with a number, believed to be the model number. Often the edge of the diaphragm is cut across three times, see illustration. This can be seen by looking through the window. It is a reliable feature for identifying this manufacturer. In 1871 the company's name change from 'Son' to 'Sons'.

Left: *Stevens & Sons overlabels. Left; 'Stevens & Sons Porteous's Whistle Southwark B'Road'. Right; 'Stevens & Sons Manufacturers London & Glasgow'.*

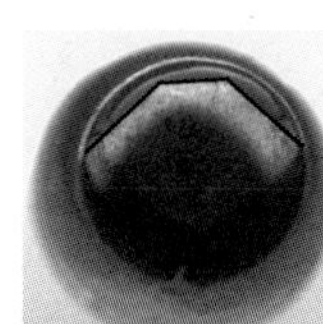

Above: *Stevens & Sons. View through the window, showing how the diaphragm is cut across in three places – a reliable identification feature.*

Stevens & Sons nickel silver round whistles, nineteenth century. Left; slide whistle marked '36' above the window. Centre left; maker's overlabel at back, marked '63' above the window. Centre right; high quality call with acorn top, maker's overlabel at back and vulcanite(?) fipple, length 66mm. Right; marked '31' above the oval window, maker's overlabel at back. All rare.

R A WALTON

R A Walton made round pea whistles but none have been positively identified.

T YATES

Thomas Yates' complete whistle catalogue of 1870 is reproduced on pages 49 and 50. It gives 87 round pea whistles made in a variety of alloys; crown metal, brass, nickel silver (German silver). Most could be supplied electro plated. This total includes whistles whose tops are figured as a dog's or bird's head, animal's hoof or claw, swan, hand or soldier's head. Five of them could be supplied gilt plated. A great number of the round whistles a collector comes across will have been made by T Yates and some are impressed 'TY' or 'T Yates', usually along the side of the body, more infrequently above the window.

T Yates marketed models which are clearly made from two individual whistles simply joined together. In addition to the 1870 catalogue some further whistles are illustrated below.

T Yates nineteenth century round whistles. Left to right: brass with brass two-hole fipple, length 49mm; Britannia metal with round mouthpiece; marked 'T Yates', Britannia metal; marked 'T Yates', Britannia metal; marked 'T Yates', Britannia metal; Britannia metal.

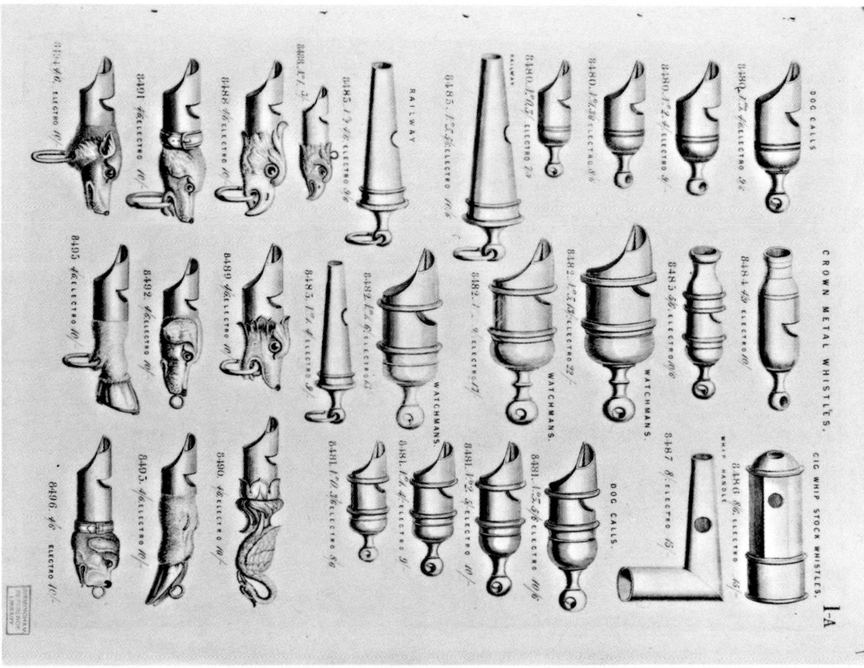

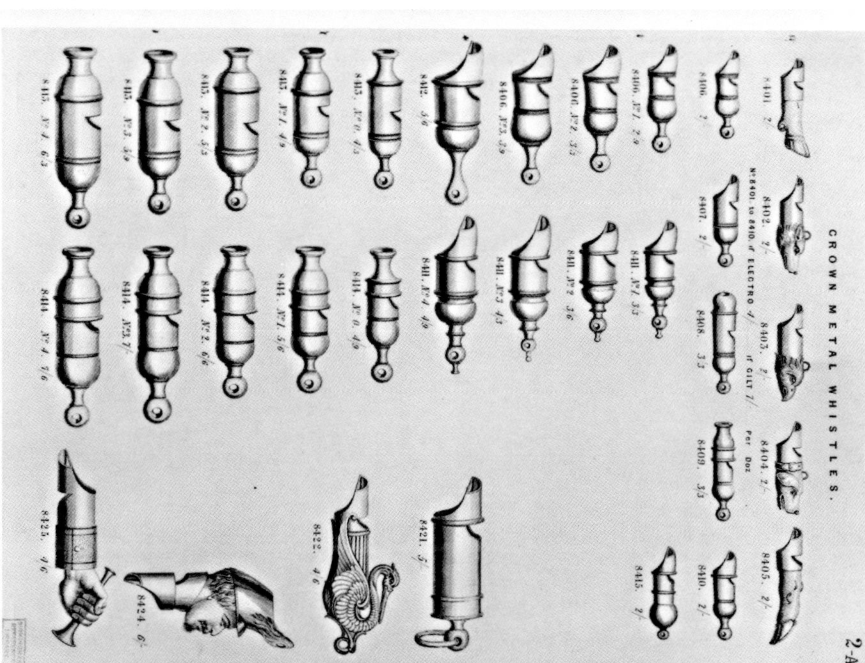

Thomas Yates catalogue 1870

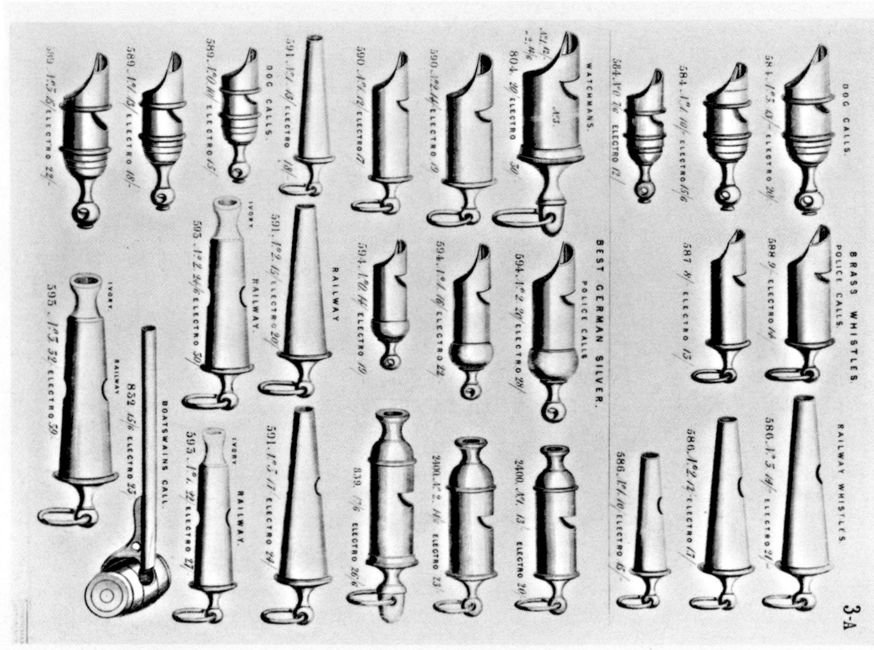

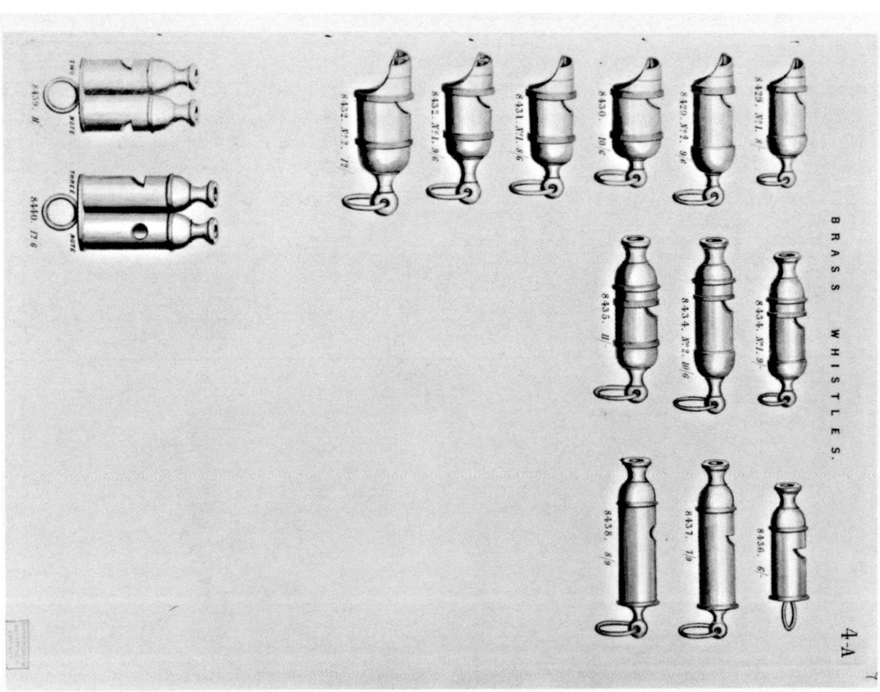

Thomas Yates catalogue 1870

T Yates nineteenth century round whistles. Left to right: body with engine turned pattern, nickel silver, length 57mm; 'NER', North Eastern Railway; 'NER', North Eastern Railway; 'TY', above the window; brass with a brass two-hole fipple; nickel silver with a black wooden fipple.

Right: *T Yates round whistle , 'L & YR Co 964 Thomas Yates Birmingham', Lancashire & Yorkshire Railway. Nickel silver, late nineteenth to early twentieth century. Rare.*

Below: *T Yates nineteenth century round whistles with round mouthpieces. Left to right: 'Stout Brs Limehouse E', nickel silver; brass body with a screw-in Britannia metal mouthpiece; nickel silver body with a Britannia metal mouthpiece; double whistle, brass body with Britannia metal top and mouthpiece; brass body with a Britannia metal top and mouthpiece.*

UNATTRIBUTED WHISTLES

The next three illustrations show round whistles without features exclusive to particular makers. Some of the features, for example, the shape of window, design of the top, the diaphragm, are common to several makers. They could have been made by S Auld, A De Courcy, T Yates, J Hudson or one of the rarer small manufacturers.

Unattributed round whistles. Left; machined from solid rod, Auld-type window, nickel plated brass, length 63mm. Centre left; military whistle with stop-hole, silver plated. Possible De Courcy, Walton or Hudson. Centre right; nickel silver, rectangular window. Right; military whistle with stop-hole, nickel silver. Reverse stamped '↑ I', British India. Possibly made by T Yates.

Unattributed round whistles. Left; gunmetal with black wooden fipple. Centre left; very large brass whistle with two-hole wooden fipple, length 67mm, width 31mm. Centre right; machined from sold nickel silver with Auld-type window and two-hole wooden fipple. Right; nickel plated brass.

Unattributed round whistles. Left; brass with plating buffed off. Centre left; smallish military call with stop-hole, nickel silver. Centre; machined gunmetal, length 72mm. Centre right; acorn-like top, nickel plated brass. Right; high quality, the design reminiscent of Coney & Co, nickel silver. Also made in a smaller size.

General service whistles

General service whistles (GSW), often referred to as 'police whistles', constitute a large number of different calls but all conform to a basic well-recognised shape. They are tube-like in appearance with two windows. The tube is internally divided lengthwise in half by a central partition. One half is slightly shorter than the other causing the whistle to produce two different notes simultaneously. The term general service whistle is preferred to 'police whistle', so as to avoid any confusion between whistles actually used by the police and those that have not—which constitute the majority. Many whistles have been, and still are, marked 'The Metropolitan' which as an 1884 trademark of J Hudson & Co and not an indication that the call was issued to the Metropolitan Police. In nearly all cases whistles issued to the various police forces are marked with the name of the force concerned, up until the last few decades of the 20th century.

Included are calls made by A De Courcy & Co and J Hudson & Co who made whistles expressly marked for railway police and referee use, and for sale by suppliers of sporting equipment. It is probable that GSW's made by other British manufacturers have at some time or another been used for sports purposes. Typical models are shown against each maker. Some have military or other markings but the whistles nevertheless exhibit typical features of the manufacturers.

ADIE BROS

Adie Bros made two GSWs during the 1939-45 conflict. Left; 'Adie Bros Birmingham 1940 ↑' nickel plated brass, length 82mm. Right; 'Adie Bros Birmingham G(crown symbol)R VI 1941'.

BENT & PARKER

Bent & Parker nickel silver GSWs. Left; 'Bent & Parker 1889 Birmingham'. This is the earliest known dated GSW by any manufacturer, length 85mm, rare. Centre left; 'Metropolitan Police', engraved at the back '15138'. Issued to the Metropolitan Police in 1885, very rare. Only about 2,000 made, making them over three times rarer than Hudson's first issue police whistle of 1884 of which approximately 7,000 were made. Centre right; 'The "Borough Whistle" Manufactured For Osborne & Son New St Birmingham', 1890s. Right; 'Bent & Parker Birmingham 1938 ↑', the most recent date known for this manufacturer.

J BARRALL

J Barrall GSWs were made between the mid 1880s and the late 1890s. Punches that were used to mark whistles with the required lettering etc, were hand cut by specialist companies. On some whistles made by J Barrall and J Hudson & Co, the lettering is so similar that clearly the same company must have been used to make the punches. Early Barrall whistles are of a lower quality than later ones.

Left: *J Barrall GSWs. Left; 'City Police', early whistle. Centre left; 'City Police', later whistle. When viewed up the mouthpiece a narrow, short rectangular piece of metal can be seen at the centre of the diaphragm. This is an extension to the partition which passes through the diaphragm, a design not recorded as being used by Barrall until now. It is a well known feature of W Dowler & Sons whistles and to a lesser extent of those by Bent & Parker, H A Ward and T Yates. Centre; plain nickel silver, length 91mm. Centre right; plain nickel plated brass. Right; 'Birmingham Police Warranted Perfect' and within an oval 'Barrall Birmingham'. All rare.*

A DE COURCY & CO

The company made whistles between 1888 and 1927.

A De Courcy & Co. Styles of two-piece tops made to Patent 101303 of 1916.

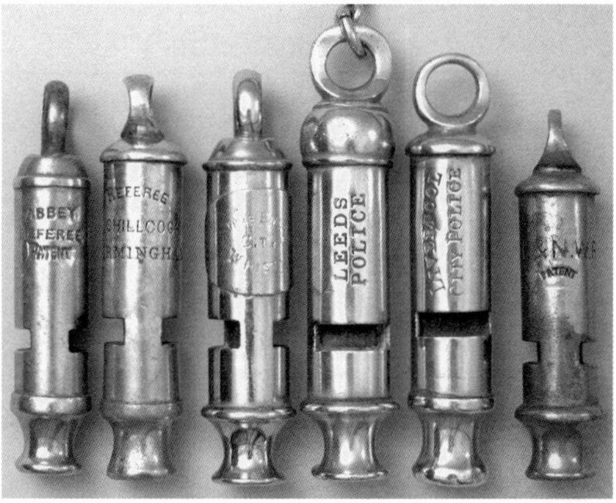

Below right: *A De Courcy & Co GSWs. Left to right; 'Abbey Referee Patent'. The patent refers to Patent 101303 of 1916 which specifies a two-piece top – normally the loop is formed from a 'D' cross section wire but it may be also made from flat strip or appear as a flat washer. The internal diaphragm is made to an earlier patent, number 17165/1913 – when viewed up the mouthpiece a folded-down strip can be seen. Abbey is a sporting goods company, length 79mm, 1916-27; 'Referee W Shillcock Birmingham', 1900s-10s; an historically important whistle – made by De Courcy before the company, and its stock, was sold to J Hudson & Co in 1927. Hudsons attached an overlabel marked 'The Emca City Whistle', very rare; 'Leeds Police' with a Porteous top, diaphragm made to Patent 3725/1906 – when viewed up the mouthpiece a line can be seen that goes from one side of the diaphragm to the other. Length 91mm,1906-c.1916; 'Liverpool City Police', with the Liver Bird crest on the opposite side, 1913-27; 'L&NWR Patent', London & North West Railway, 1906 patent.*

CASCELLOID LTD

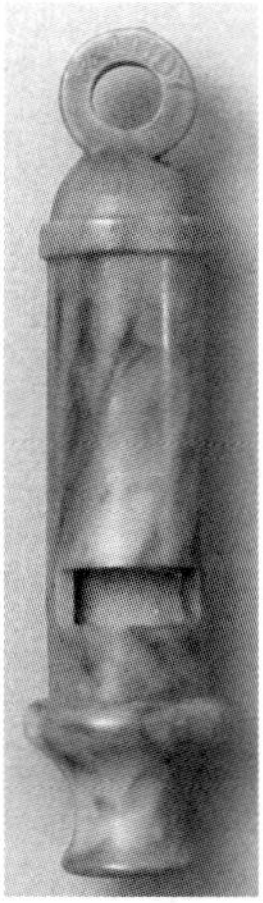

Cascelloid Ltd plastic toy GSW in mottled red, yellow & blue. Top-loop marked 'Palitoy Made In England', length 77mm, pre 1985.

CONEY & CO

Coney & Co GSWs of the 1900s. The tops and mouthpieces are of a distinctive shape. Left; 'Extra Size Central' with curved windows, length 95mm. Right; 'Coney's Alarm' with the windows at different heights along the body.

W DOWLER & SONS

W Dowler & Sons nickel silver GSWs, 1880s-1900s. They all have a short, narrow rectangular extension to the partition which passes through the diaphragm. When viewed up the mouthpiece it is visible as a narrow rectangle. Left; 'Huddersfield Police' and 'W Dowler Birmm' on the opposite side, Porteous top, length 87mm. Centre left; 'Manchester Highways Department 4', milling to the mouthpiece. Centre right; 'Dowler & Sons 94 Gt Charles St Birmingham 1894'. This is the earliest recorded dated Dowler whistle, rare. Right; 'Wakefield City Police', the squat, flat top is a Dowler characteristic.

J HUDSON & CO

J Hudson & Co GSWs. Left; heavy cast alloy model with four windows, 1930s, length 83mm. Centre; 'The Metropolitan' in walnut Bakelite with four windows, 1930s, very rare. A green example has been noted. Right; 'The Acme' in black plastic with a metal ring joining the top to the body, 1930s, very rare.

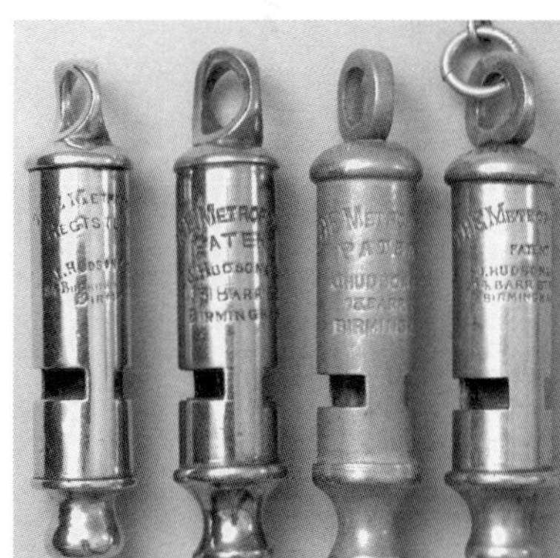

Right: *J Hudson & Co addresses. Left to right; 84 Buckingham Street, 1883-84; 131 Barr Street, 1885-88; 13 Barr Street 1888-1909; 244 Barr Street, 1909 onwards.*

Right: *J Hudson & Co GSWs. Left; early small size model, 63mm, 1900s. Centre left; cheap toy model, plated steel body, 1930s. Centre right; single note call with a pea, plated steel, 1930s. Right; 'The Emca', a 1922 trademark, inexpensive range of whistles, 1920s-30s. Examples later than 1939 have a 'pip' at the circumference of the diaphragm opposite each window.*

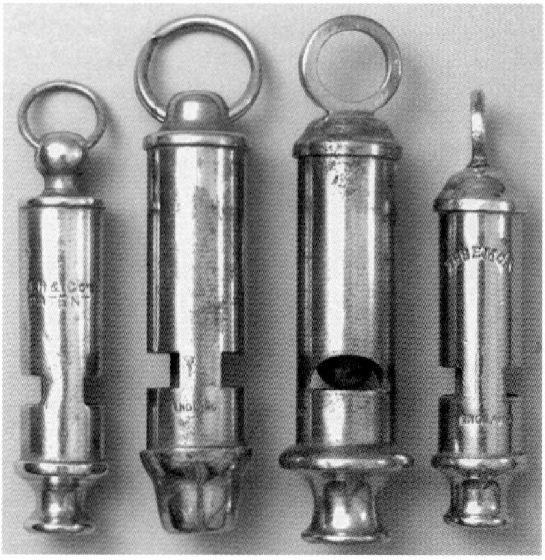

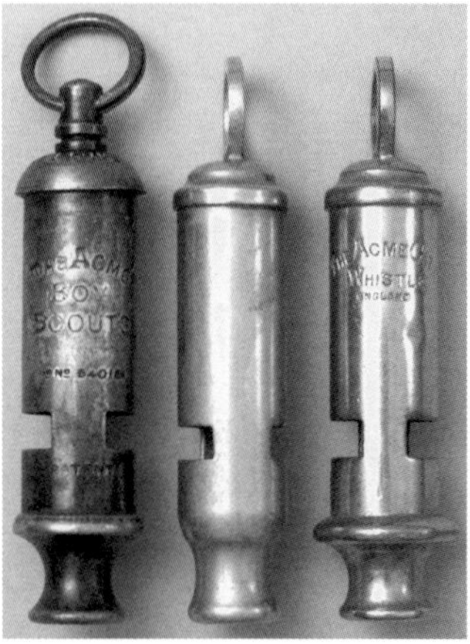

Left: *J Hudson & Co GSWs. Left; 'The Acme Boy Scouts Rd No 540164'. The Acme Boy Scouts became a trademark in 1909 and the registered design number relates to the pillar top, also from 1909. Cap marked 'Patent 5727·08', the patent for a top made in two pieces, 1909-22. Centre; whistle with the mouthpiece and body made from a single component, Patent 28999/1911, valid until 1925. This example from the 1930s. Right; 'The Acme City Whistle England'. a lightweight inexpensive call with a typical bulbous looking mouthpiece of the 1930s and 40s, this example 1930s.*

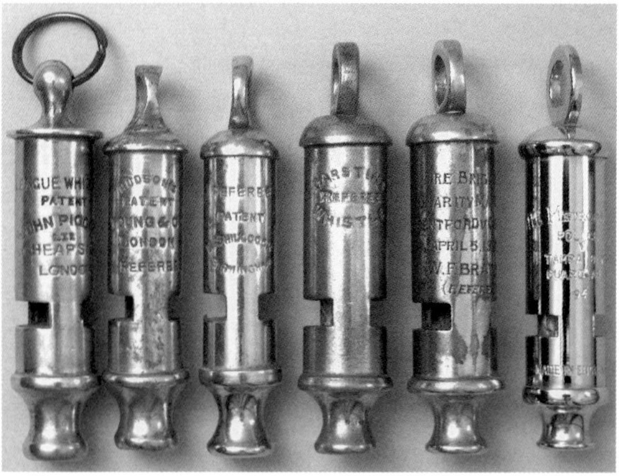

Left: *J Hudson & Co GSWs. Left to right; 'League Whistle Patent John Piggott Ltd Cheapside London', 1910s; 'Hudson's Patent Young & Co London Referee', 1890s; 'Referee Patent W Shillcock Birmingham', 1920s; 'Garstins Referee Whistle', 1910s; an Acme City Whistle engraved, 'Fire Brigade Charity Match Brentford v Chiswick April 5, 1920. W F Brown (Referee)'; 'The Metropolitan Police v Tampa Bay Guardians 94', Only 100 made in 1994.*

Right: *J Hudson & Co GSWs. Left; 'The Acme Registered Hudson's Patent', the patent referred to is 435/1885 for a diaphragm design – the top of the diaphragm is marked 'Hudsons Patent' and is visible through the windows. A large call with domed cap and hollow spherical knop, plated brass, 1890s, length 90mm. Right; 'The Kinglet', a large whistle manufactured for many years, this example 1908 to the early 1920s. Steel body with brass mouthpiece and top.*

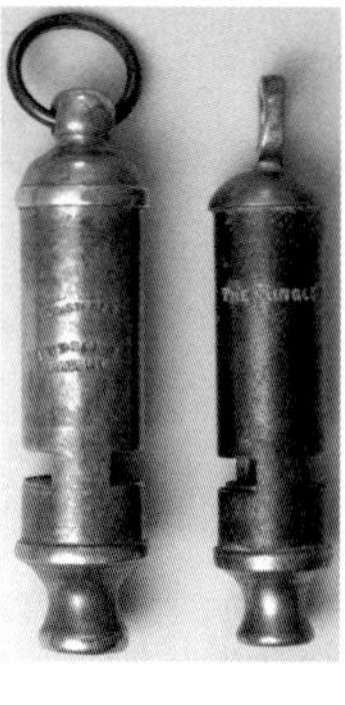

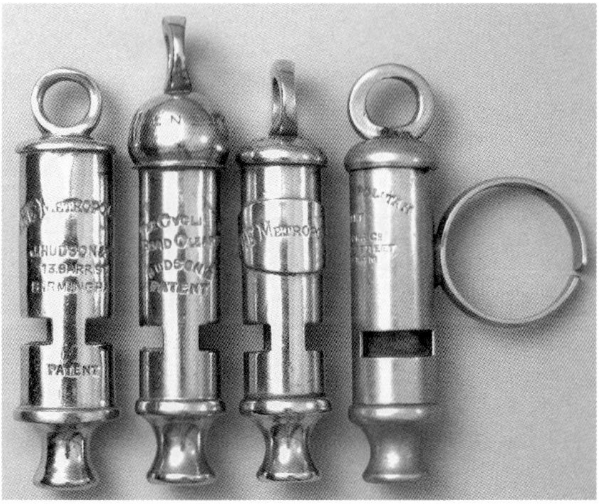

Left: *J Hudson & Co GSWs. Left; oval model made for many years. This example marked 'Patent', relating to 19700/1898. This coupled with the 13 Barr Street address, vacated in 1909, dates the whistle between 1898 and 1909. Centre left; 'The Cyclists Road Clearer' with a two-piece Porteous top marked 'Patent No 5727-08'. A splendid call of the early 20th century, 91mm, rare. Earlier examples, pre-1908, would have a top cast in one piece. Centre right; 'The Metropolitan' on an overlabel. Overlabels were a method of covering up unwanted or cancelled markings thus making the whistle saleable. Right; whistle with a finger ring enabling it to be worn on a gloved hand. Known as the cavalry model.*

Right: *J Hudson & Co GSWs. 'The Acme Referee' became a trademark in 1908 but usage ceased before 1939. Left; 'The Acme Referee', top-cap marked 'Hudson's Patent 5727·08'. This style of cap marking was used for only a year or so, making this whistle one of the first Acme Referees. Centre left; 'The Acme Referee' with a rare design of top, 1930s. Centre; 'The Acme Referee', black oxidised finish and pillar top (usually reserved for scouting whistles). Centre right & right; 'Regd Bukta', a sports company. Larger call 'B2', smaller 'B1'.*

Left: *J Hudson & Co railway police GSWs. Left; 'L&NWR', London & North Western Railway, 1910s. Centre left; 'LB&SCR', London Brighton & South Coast Railway, 1908-09. This whistle can be dated within two years as the top-cap is made to a 1908 patent and the address on the whistle, 13 Barr St, changed in 1909. Centre; 'L&NER', London & North Eastern Railway, 1930s. Centre right; 'LMS', London, Midland, Scottish Railway. Marked on a cheaper range of whistle, 1930s. Right; 'BR (M)', British Railways Midlands, 1960s.*

DATING J HUDSON & CO GENERAL SERVICE WHISTLES Chart No.1

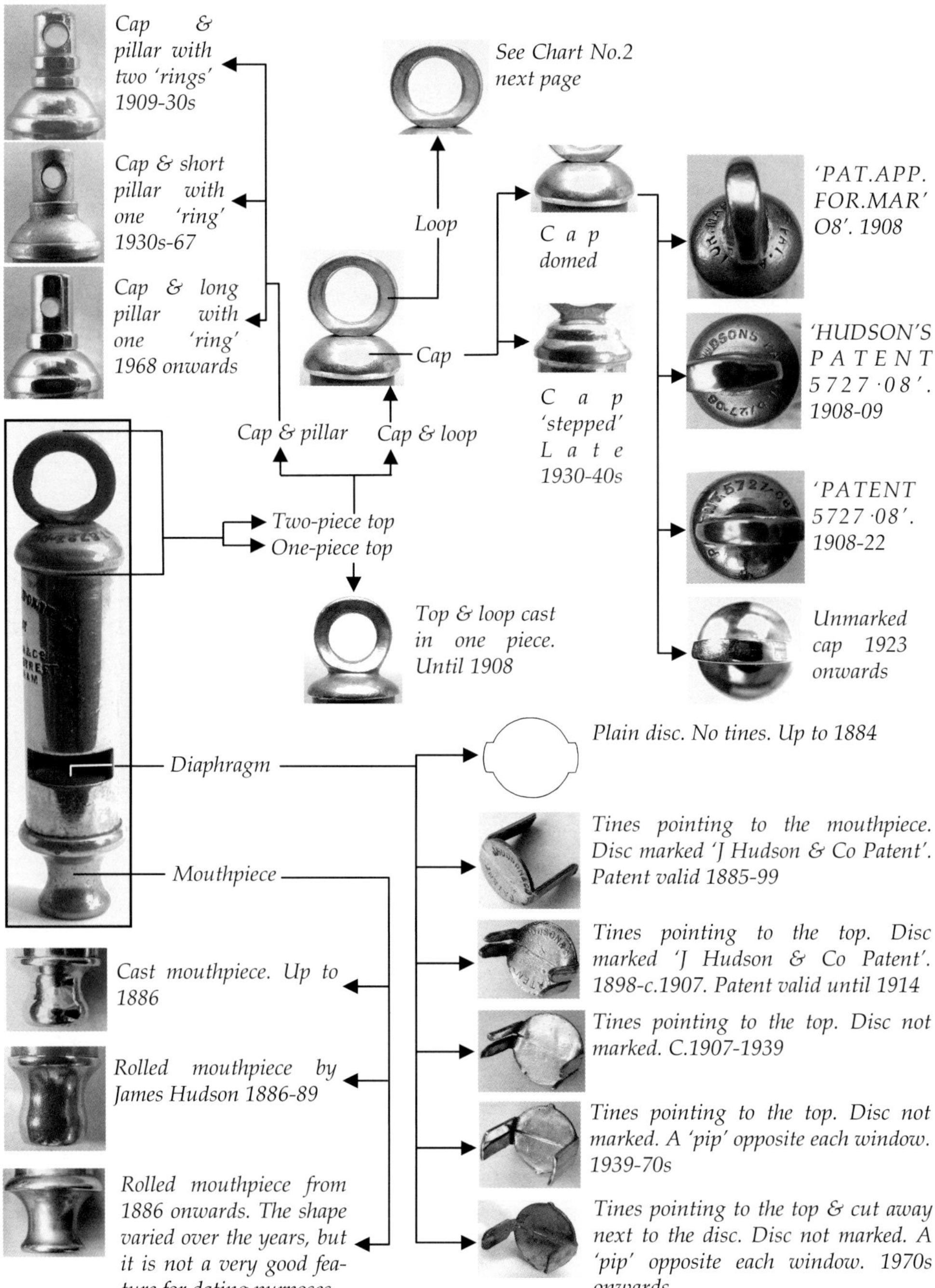

DATING J HUDSON & CO GENERAL SERVICE WHISTLES Chart No.2

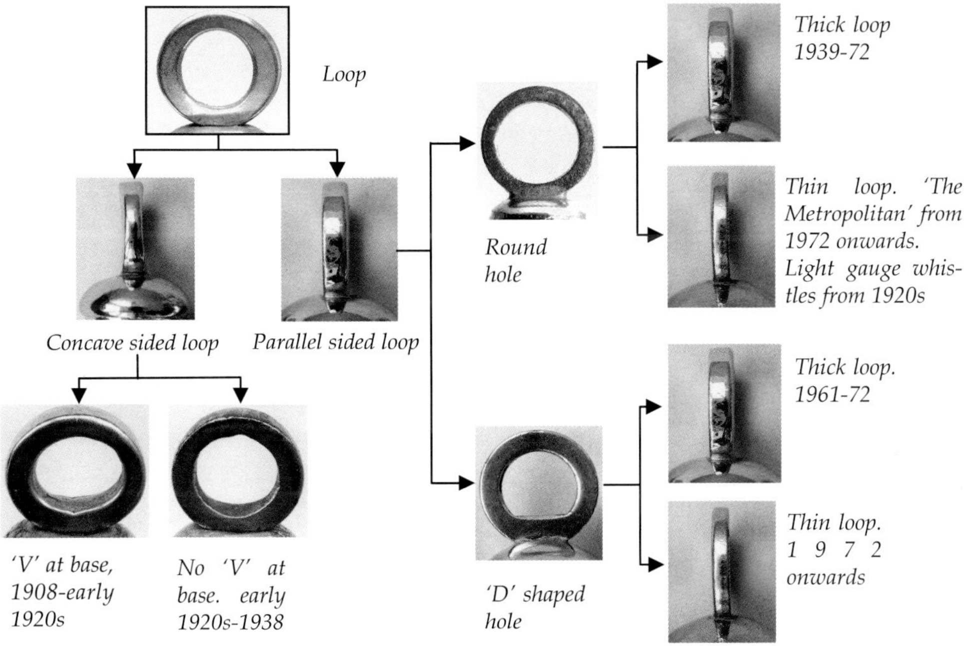

B LILLY & SONS

B Lilly & Sons retailed whistles made by other manufacturers. The calls can be recognised by the fact that the top loop is at right angles to the window—normally this component is in line with the windows. An illustration of such a whistle is shown under T Yates.

H W SHORT

Whistles by H W Short are easily identified as they were marked 'Short's Twopiece'. They were made in two pieces which when pushed together held firmly. One piece comprises of the body and mouthpiece, the other of the top, and internal diaphragm and partition. All calls by H W Short are exceptionally rare.

STADIUM LTD

Stadium Ltd were motor car accessoreies manufacturers who briefly made GSWs in 1941.

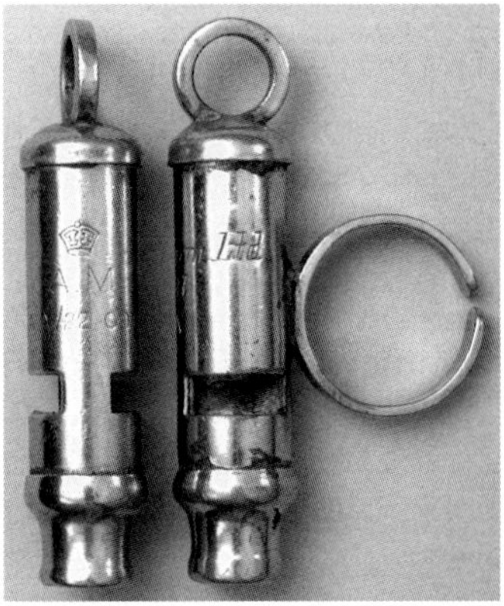

Stadium Ltd. Left; '(crown symbol) AM 293/AA/22 CON.14C', nickel plated brass, length 81mm. Right; 'Stadium Ltd 1940↑', with 30mm diameter finger-ring.

STEVENS & SONS

An important manufacturer of high quality whistles from the early 19th century and probably the inventors of the Porteous top—an almost spherical top. In 1871 the name of the company changed from 'Son' to 'Sons'. The mouthpieces of their early GSWs unscrew to reveal that the diaphragm and mouthpiece have been machined from a single piece of metal. This is a distinctive identifying feature.

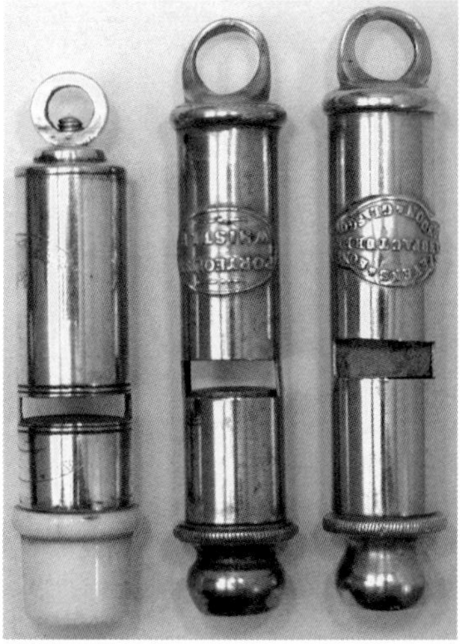

Stevens & Sons GSWs. Left; early 19th century single note call, silver plated brass with an ivory mouthpiece, length 77mm, very rare. Centre; 'Porteous's Whistle' on an overlabel, single note call, nickel plated brass, 1860s or earlier, very rare. Right; 'Stevens & Sons Manufacturers London & Glasgow' on an overlabel, nickel silver, 1870s, very rare.

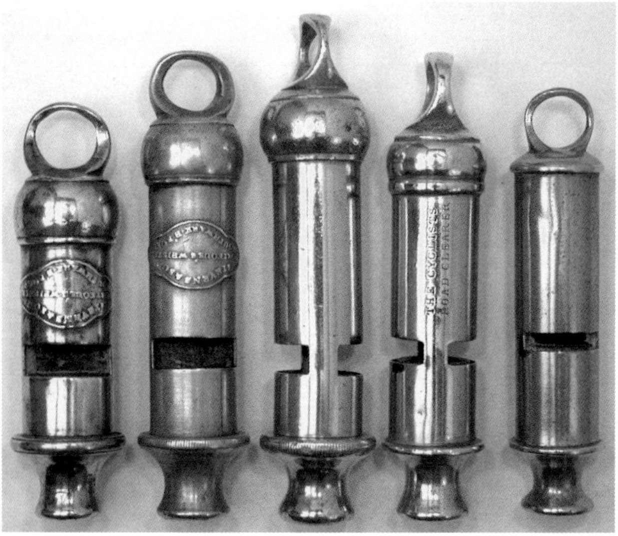

Stevens & Sons. Distinctive mouthpiece and diaphragm machined out of a single piece of metal.

Stevens & Sons GSWs. Left to right; 'Stevens & Son Porteous's Whistle Southwark B'Road' on an overlabel, brass, very rare; 'Stevens & Son Porteous's Whistle Southwark B'Road' on an overlabel. On the other side of the whistle is punched '27', probably the model number. Pre-1870, very rare; Large impressive whistle, unmarked, but identified as by Stevens through its combined mouthpiece and diaphragm. Length 96mm, 19th century, nickel silver, very rare; 'The Cyclist Road Clearer' 'HAK & Co London'. H A Knox was a London supplier of cycle accessories from 1870, nickel silver. A much sought after whistle. Examples of this whistle were also made stamped 'Knox's Improved Police Call'; Unmarked nickel plated brass, distinctive by having narrow windows high up the body.

Left: *Stevens & Sons overlabels. Left; 'Porteous's Whistle'. Centre; 'Stevens & Sons Manufacturers London & Glasgow'. Right; 'Stevens & Son Porteous's Whistle Southwark B'Road'.*

R A WALTON

R A Walton GSWs, 1898-1904, nickel plated brass. Left; 'The Universal City Police', length 81mm. The Universal was a Walton brand name. Right; 'Provisional Protection No 10492'. A patent diaphragm design of 1898.

H A WARD

H A Ward GSW. 'The Standard Police Or Fire H Arthur Ward Birmingham', nickel plated brass, length 88mm. Difficult to find.

T YATES

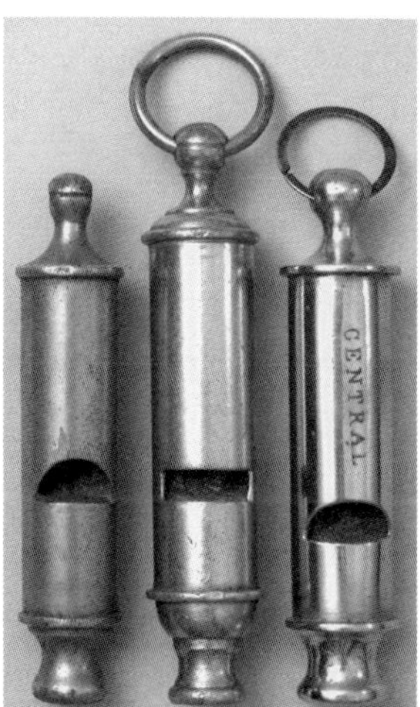

Left: *Thomas Yates GSWs. Nickel plated brass, before 1910s. Right; marked 'Central', length 79mm.*

Right: *Thomas Yates GSW. Nickel plated brass, loop at right angles to the window. This is a distinctive feature of whistles made for B Lilly & Sons. Length 82mm, 1900s.*

Multi-tube & multi–chambered whistles

MULTI-TUBE WHISTLES

Multi-tube whistles are constructed from two or more tubes of varying length joined to a single mouthpiece. They can be divided into two main groups; either with an in-line mouthpiece or with the mouthpiece at an angle to the tubes. Both types were advertised as cyclists whistles until the 1920s, but no doubt they were used for refereeing and umpiring during this period. Later advertising pointed out their special sports potential made possible through using a number of different models, each producing a different sound. Contemporary advertising proclaimed that several games of hockey, for example, could take place next to each other without confusion, with players being able to recognise which whistle amongst several to respond to if each umpire had a different model.

MULTI-CHAMBERED WHISTLES

Multi-chambered whistles are those that have more than one sounding chamber within the body of the call.

A DE COURCY & CO

'The Champion' by A De Courcy & Co was a two-tube angled mouthpiece pattern in four sizes ranging in length from 70mm to 120mm. De Courcys also made a two-tube in-line whistle, as shown below.

A De Courcy & Co multi-tube whistle with in-line mouthpiece, late 19th to early 20th century, plated brass, length 88mm.

J DIXON & SONS

James Dixon & Sons two-chambered Britannia metal call, length 51mm. There is an identical whistle marked 'Sykes', the well-known powder flask maker, which was probably made for them by Dixons.

J HUDSON & CO

J Hudson & Co made multi-tube whistles with angled and in-line mouthpieces, and multi-chambered calls. Each class of whistle is described in turn.

ANGLED MOUTHPIECE MODELS

Advertised from the 1900s was 'The Universal'; multi-tube whistles with angled mouthpieces. They were aimed at cyclists and sports umpires, but in the mid 1940s the name changed to 'The Acme'. The tubes were manufactured in a single piece by drawing down the centre of a flat disc of metal into a tube. From the early

1970s they were made from cut lengths of tubing with the ends capped with plugs, and the mouthpieces were struck 'Acme Regd'. Over the years they have been available with two, three and four tubes, and in various sizes. For example, from the mid 1930s through to the 1950s the two-tube model was made in four sizes (64, 76, 89 & 115mm), the three-tube in two sizes (67 & 102mm) and the four-tube in a single size (89mm). Additionally, during the 1930s a saliva guard could be fitted. The number of models has steadily decreased and the sizes have undergone various changes until at the beginning of the 2000s only two, two-tube metal patterns were available.

Plastic multi-tube whistles were produced by Hudsons in assorted colours from the late 1940s until c.1970. The range consisted of a three-tube pattern and two, two-tube patterns. In 1989 a plastic three-tube whistle was launched as part of Hudson's 'Tornado' range of whistles. It is not affected by water, operates in sub-zero temperatures and utters an impressive sound.

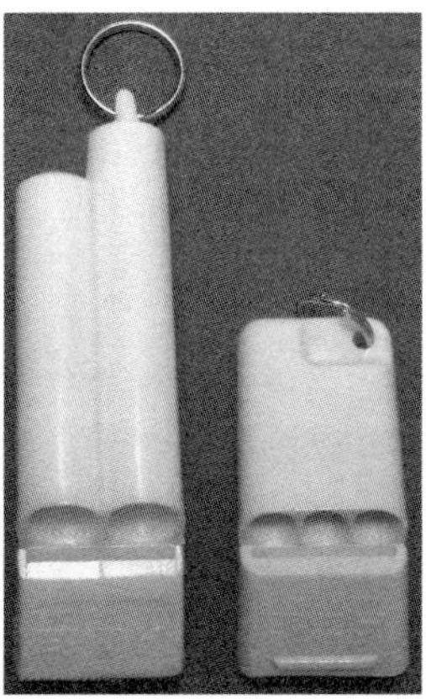

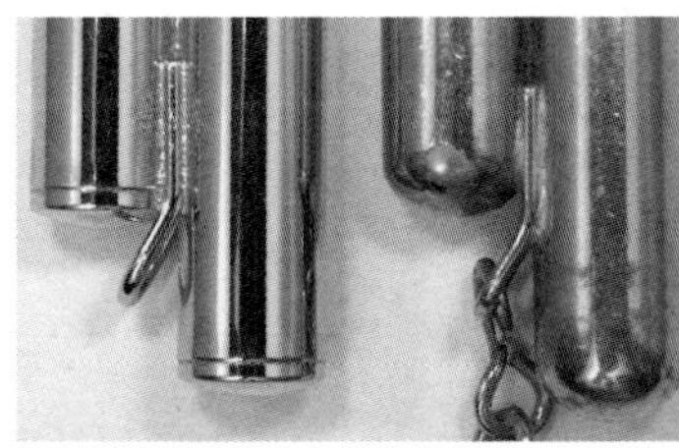

Right: *J Hudson & Co multi-tube whistles with angled mouthpieces. Left; the end of the tube is capped with a plug, from the 1970s. Right; the tube and end are in one piece, before the early 1970s. Note: The end of the tube for multi-tube whistles with in-line mouthpieces changed from one-piece to a plug in the 1940s.*

Above: *J Hudson & Co plastic multi-tube whistles with angled mouthpieces. Left; 'Acme Made In England', 2-tube, late 1940s-c.1970, made in an assortment of colours, rare. A 3-tube pattern was also made. Right; 'Acme Made In England', 3-tube in moulded plastic from 1989 onwards, length 50mm. From 1992 made only in international safety orange or black but originally also in blue, yellow, red and white.*

Below: *J Hudson & Co multi-tube whistles with angled mouthpieces advertised for cyclists and sports umpires. Left top; mouthpiece marked 'BMMO', Birmingham and Midland Motor Omnibus Co, 3-tube 1940s to early 1970s. Left centre; 'The Acme Made In England', 3-tube, 1940s to early 1970s, length 102mm. Left bottom; 'The Acme England', 4-tube, 1940s. Right top; 'The Universal Call', 2-tube, 1900s-30s. Right centre; 'The Universal Call', 2-tube, 1900s-30s. Right bottom; 'Acme Regd Made In England', 2-tube, early 1970s onwards.*

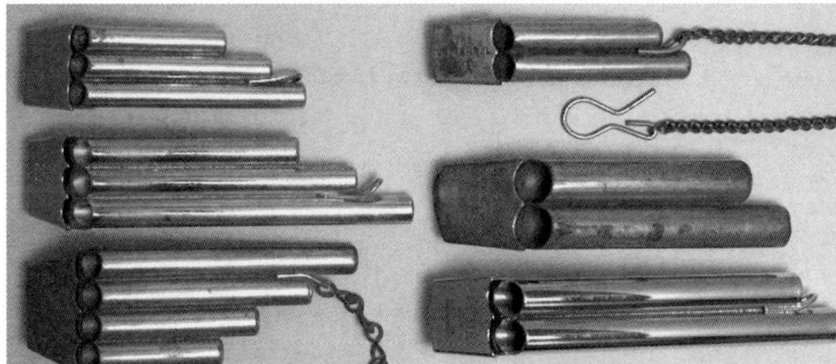

IN-LINE MOUTHPIECE MODELS

J Hudson & Co fabricated multi-tube whistles with in-line mouthpieces from the end of the nineteenth century. They were made to cater for the needs of cyclists and umpires. The earliest that has been noted was manufactured utilising Patent 435 of 1885—this patent has the tines of the diaphragm pointing towards the mouthpiece. Apart from this very first model, illustrated below, subsequent productions were seventy six millimetres long until an additional model at eighty nine millimetres was added in the 1930s. The two continued until the smaller one was dropped in the 1950s, and finally production ceased in the early 1970s. Early examples have the tubes formed by drawing out a tube from a disc of metal, but from the 1940s they were made from tubing cut to length, the ends closed with a cap.

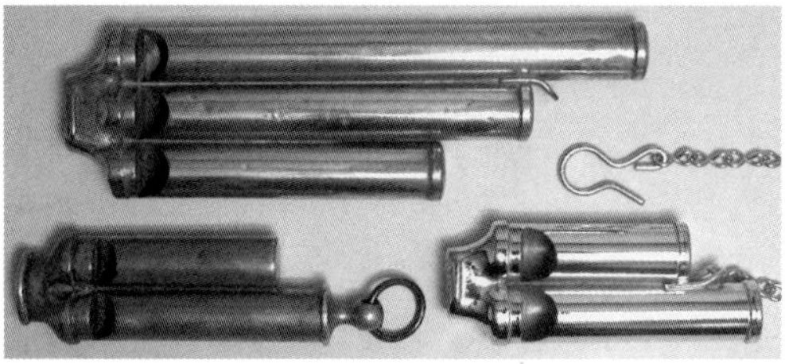

Below: *J Hudson & Co. Top; ocean liner or American railroad effects, with black plastic mouthpiece, 1930s-90s, length 315mm. Earlier examples exist with walnut Bakelite mouthpieces, rare. Bottom: Left; tug boat or Mississippi Steamer effects call with black plastic mouthpiece, 1930s-90s, length 165mm. Right; same model at before but with a metal mouthpiece, 1940s-70s.*

Above: *J Hudson & Co multi-tube whistles with in-line mouthpieces. Top; 3-tube, 142mm, 1930s. Left; 2-tube, earliest recorded example utilising Hudson's first patent diaphragm design, 1885-99. Right; end cap marked 'Made In England', 1950s.*

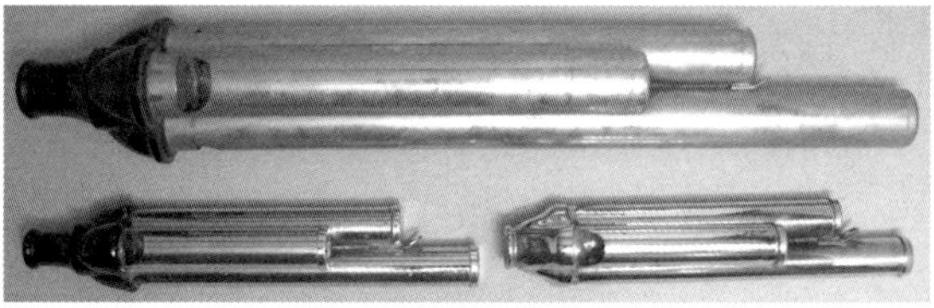

MULTI-CHAMBERED MODELS

Hudson's made a two-chambered whistle from 1909 until the 1970s called 'The Acme Taxi-Call'. It was made to Patent 553 of 1909 and made an important advance in the construction of whistles. Its significance lies in the plate which is part of the fipple and forms the underside of the mouthpiece. Previously this plate was simply soldered to the body of the whistle but in the new design it also interlocked at three points. This design is illustrated on page 43. Hudson's have used this design on all their round pea whistles since 1909 and it thus provides the collector with a convenient identification and dating characteristic.

In 1989 a range of pealess plastic whistles called the 'Tornado' was introduced, supplemented later on with the 'Tornado 2000'. They have several separate chambers within the body connected to a single mouthpiece. The range is comprised of, (a) an unmistakable angled mouthpiece multi-tube whistle, illustrated on the previous page (b) a flat whistle, when viewed in profile, (c) three escargot-like calls. These when viewed from the side clearly look like escargot whistles, but what would have been the ends of the barrel in a traditional escargot now function only as a place to grip the whistle. The largest has a straight sided mouthpiece, the others tapered, and (d) the 'Tornado 2000', a large robust call. Some of the range may be fitted with finger grips and early examples have a solid back and an angled profile. The range has been made in assorted plain colours and bi-colour. Bi-colour whistles have a different colour front and back.

The final plastic escargot is the attractive looking 'Acme Cyclone 888' launched in the 1990s. It has an escargot profile but is a two-chambered pealess whistle made in an assortment of colours.

J Hudson & Co two-chambered whistles. Left; large size in buffalo horn, length 71mm, 1900s. Also made in a medium and small size. Centre left; oval nickel silver call made from rod, late 19th to early 20th century. Centre right; 'The Acme Taxi-Call'. This whistle was made to Patent 553 of 1909, valid until 1923, and included a 3-point interlocking mouthpiece plate at the back. This is perhaps the most useful feature in putting many of Hudsons whistles into a manufacturing period. Whistles without an interlocking plate date before 1908. With the plate marked 'Patent' between 1909 and 1923, and those with an unmarked plate from 1924 onwards. Right; taxi-call model 'The Acme England LNER', 1930s-60s.

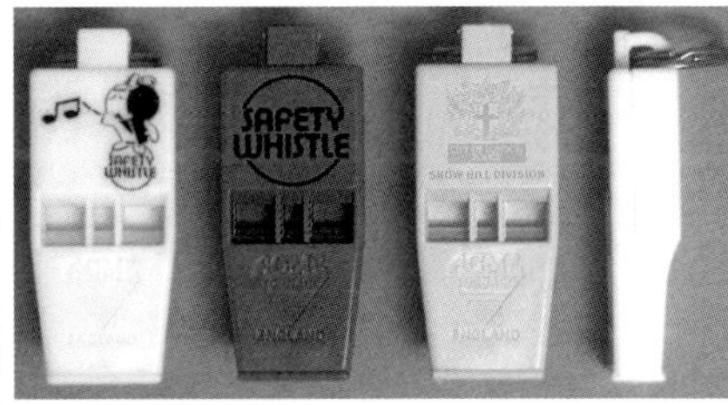

J Hudson & Co triple-chambered whistles, length 50mm, early examples 1989-91. 'Acme Tornado England' below the window. Later whistles marked above the window. All marked at the back 'SOLAS Approved Pat. Pend'. SOLAS stands for Saving Of Life At Sea. Centre right; 'City of London Police Snow Hill', issued as part of a neighbourhood watch scheme.

J Hudson & Co 'Acme Tornado'. Left; early 'smooth' back. Right; more recent back.

J Hudson & Co multi-chambered plastic calls. Left; 'Acme Tornado 2000', 3-chambered escargot-like whistle, length 49mm. Centre left; 'Acme Cyclone 888', 2-chambered, 1990s. Centre; 'Acme Tornado' above the window, with parallel sided mouthpiece. Top green, bottom yellow – an assortment of colour combinations were made from 1991. Centre right; early 'Acme Tornado'. Marked below the window, tapered mouthpiece, 1989-91. Back of the whistle made 'smooth' by means of an additional piece, see illustration above right. Right; 'Acme Tornado' above the window, tapered mouthpiece, 1991 onwards.

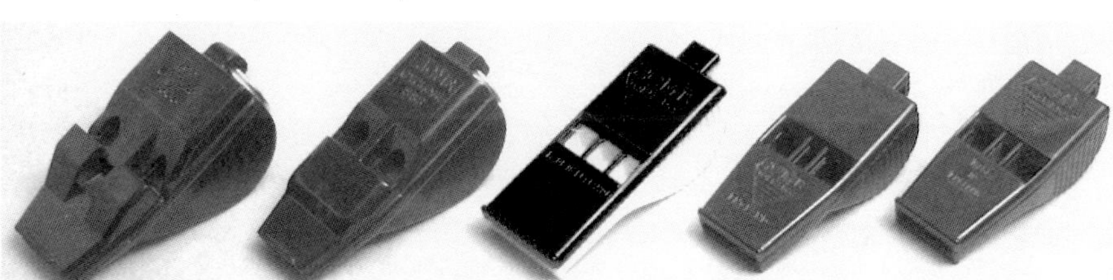

J Hudson & Co black plastic 'Acme Tornado' with tapering mouthpiece and finger grips. A 3-chambered escargot-like whistle made from 1989 onwards, length 50mm.

D LEWIS

In 1916 D Lewis was granted Patent 107442 for a three-tube call with an angled mouthpiece which had tubes of the same length. However, each tube was blanked off inside at different points thus effectively causing the call to produce three different notes. Examples of Lewis's Triphone are unknown.

B LILLY & SONS

In c.1910 B Lilly & Sons sold an angled mouthpiece model called 'The Lilly'. They also sold the 'Speedwell' range with in-line mouthpieces believed to have been manufactured by H A Ward.

Above: *B Lilly & Sons multi-tube whistles with angled mouthpieces. Marked 'The Lilly', overall lengths 73mm & 79mm, plated brass, c.1910s. Rare.*

STEVENS & SONS

Left: *Stevens & Son. 'Porteus's Instrument For Signals Registered February 27 1845'. Upper; four-tube, length 90mm. Lower; three-tube. Both very rare.*

Right: *Multi-tube whistle with in-line mouthpiece, possibly made by J Barrall, c.1890s, length 83mm.*

H A WARD

Right: *Multi-tube whistles with in-line mouthpieces believed to have been made by H A Ward. Although they do not bear his name there are similarities between these and whistles known to have been made by him. All are plated brass. Left to right; 'Improved Speedwell', Length 82mm; 'Speedwell', mouthpiece with tooth-grips; 'Speedwell', mouthpiece without tooth-grips; 'The City Whistle'. 1900s.*

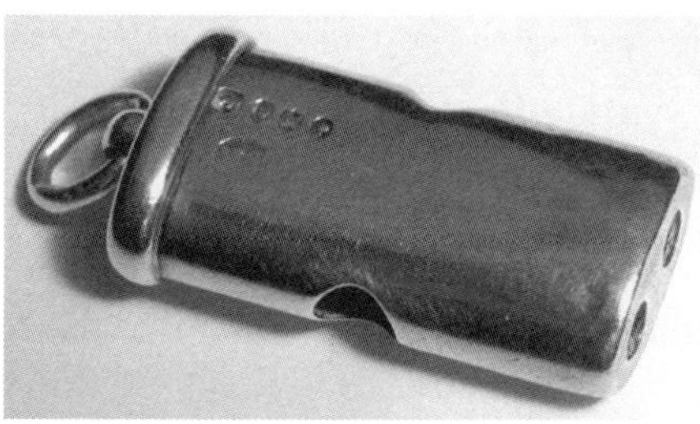

Left: *Two-chambered oval silver whistle. Hallmarks for London, 1887, sponsor's mark 'WS', length 40mm.*

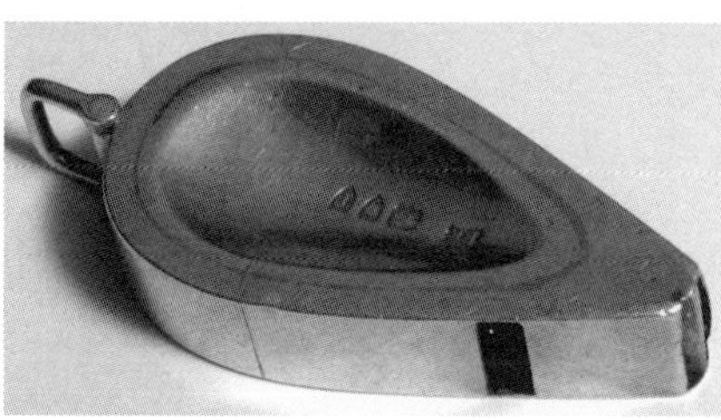

Left: *Two-chambered teardrop shaped silver whistle. Hallmarks for London, 1894, sponsor's mark 'FE', length 55mm.*

Clockwise from top left; Two-chambered round horn whistle, diameter 28mm; ivory two-chambered rectangular whistle; bone two chambered whistle.

Composite whistles

The composite whistle is a call constructed from two whistles joined top-to-top. They were advertised by suppliers for the use of cyclists, dog owners and by the disciplined services, including the Royal Navy and fire brigades.

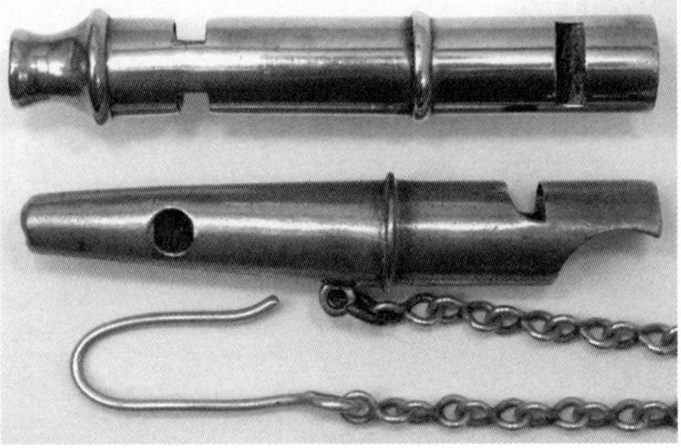

A De Courcy & Co composite whistles. Top; general service and round whistle, plated brass, 1900s, length 100mm, rare. Bottom; Beaufort and round pea whistle, 1920s, rare. This pattern also made in a smaller size. The curve to the underside of the round whistles' mouthpiece is greater than Hudsons equivalent and the window of the Beaufort is nearer to the front. De Courcys made a further two sizes of a call made from a Beaufort whistle combined with a tapering round pea whistle.

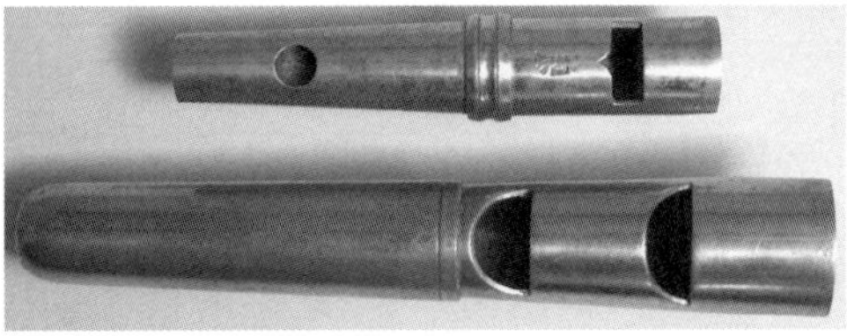

James Dixon & Sons high quality composite whistles, 1880s. Top; Beaufort and round whistle, marked 'Dixon & Sons' and with their trumpet and banner trademark. Advertised as a railway whistle with a dog-call. Bottom; horn and round whistle advertised as a call for cyclists use, length 123mm, rare.

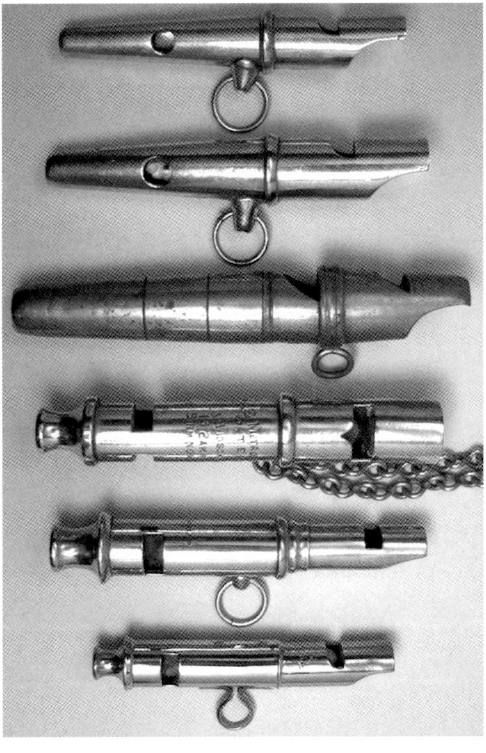

J Hudson & Co composite whistles. Top to bottom: 1930s-40s, length 95mm; 1930s-40s, length 104mm; tapered round whistle with cyclist's horn, early 20th century; 'Metropolitan' with a round whistle, notched window and 100cm 'gunner's chain', Registered Design 256361 of 1895. This example 1895-1909. This pattern was supplied to the Royal Navy's Motor Torpedo Boat Service in the early 20th century. No examples have been seen bearing either the registered design number or the government's broad arrow mark. The name, 'Torpedo Boat Service whistle' is often used to describe all whistles of this pattern regardless of age; shortish 1930s general service whistle with a small 1900s round whistle; small composite whistle, 1950s-60s.

Left: *J Hudson & Co composite whistle. Silver general service whistle combined with a round 'pea' whistle. Inlaid with an enamelled flag for the Eastern Telegraph Company, London shippers. Hallmarks for 1914. Very rare.*

Below: *W Dowler & Sons composite whistle, 1890s, nickel silver, length 106mm. 'Dowler & Sons 94 Gt Charles St Birmingham'. It is believed Dowler's never made round whistles and the one used here was probably made by De Courcy & Co.*

Above: *B Lilly & Sons. They were suppliers and manufacturers of whistles in the 1900s. The Beaufort whistle is marked 'Police Or Fire', and the round whistle 'Game Keeper', plated brass, length 100mm. Rare.*

Below: *T Yates composite whistles, late 19th to early 20th century. Top; 'T Yates', Britannia metal, length 80mm. Centre; Britannia metal. Bottom; plated brass.*

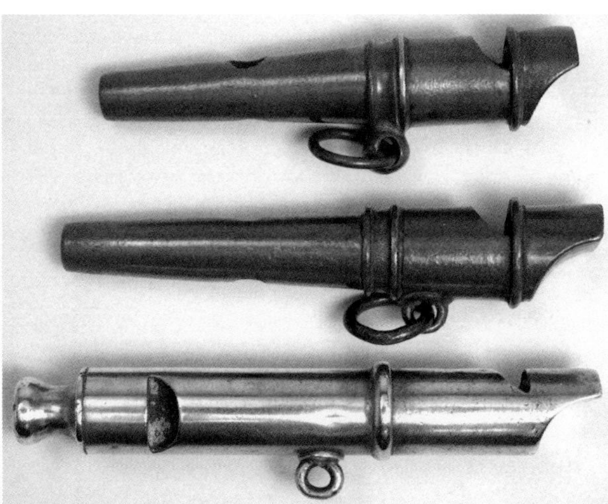

Right: *R A Walton composite whistle. Beaufort and round whistle. 'Liverpool Police', plated brass, 1890s, length 104mm. Very rare.*

Sportsmen in the countryside

Dogs respond well to high-pitched whistles, and any such call would be suitable for dog training. However, if the whistle is lost the replacement should produce an identical note as dogs learn to answer to a particular pitch. To meet this need J Hudson & Co made a range of calls manufactured to fixed pitches, plus a model which could be tuned by the owner—the 'silent' dog whistle. This last whistle was based on research by Professor Sir Frances Galton, a cousin of Charles Darwin, who found that dogs could hear sounds beyond the human range. The whistle may be tuned within, or beyond the human range. For the professional shepherd other patterns were made which combined together several whistles.

Whistles combined with a cartridge extractor were made for sporting pursuits and they were also merged with several other gun tools. Whistles were incorporated into dog and kennel whips, but identifying maker and date of manufacture is not possible with many. Most identifications are limited to the name of the supplier and to dating those with silver hallmarks or an inscription.

J DIXON & SONS

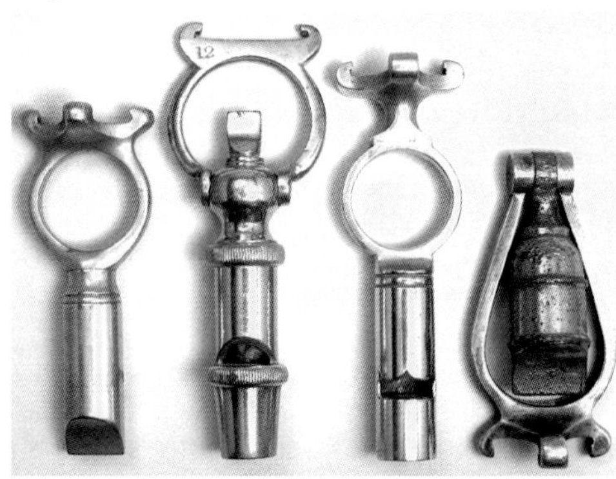

Right: *J Dixon & Sons cartridge extractors, late 19th to early 20th century. Left; 16-gauge, length 83mm. Centre left; 12-gauge, with screwdriver and nipple key. Centre right; 'James Dixon & Sons 12', nickel silver. Right; '12 Dixon & Sons' with trumpet and banner trademark. Plated brass folding extractor with Britannia metal whistle.*

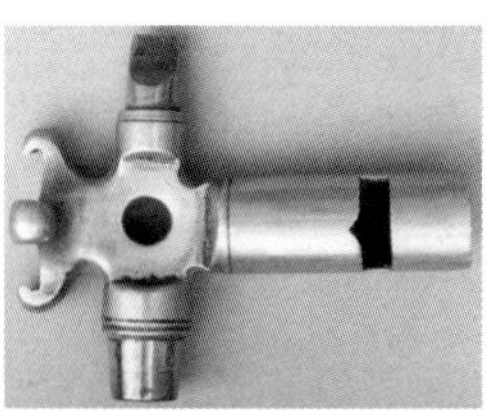

Left: *J Dixon & Sons shooter's gadget with cartridge extractor, screwdriver and nipple key, 1880s, length 70mm. Rare.*

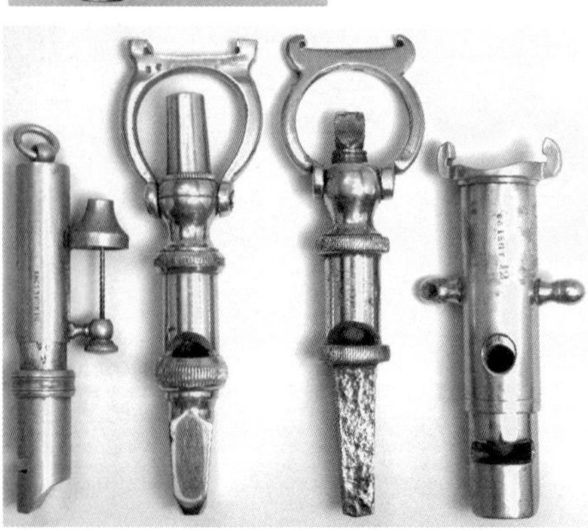

Left: *J Dixon & Sons shooter's gadgets with dog calls. Left; 'Dixon & Sons'. Powder primer with outside self-acting picker for gun nipples, 1880s, rare. Centre left; 12-gauge extractor with screwdriver and cover (shown in place) and key, late 19th century, rare. Centre right; 12-gauge extractor with screwdriver and steel key. Right; 12-gauge extractor and bird-killing blade made to Moffatt's Patent 11396/1887, rare.*

Below: *J Dixon & Sons model 104N, powder primer with inside self-acting picker for musket nipples with dog call, 1880s, length 75mm, rare.*

G & J W HAWKSLEY

G & J W Hawksley 12-gauge cartridge extractors, late 19th to early 20th century. Centre right is rigid and nickel silver, length 87mm, the others folding and plated brass.

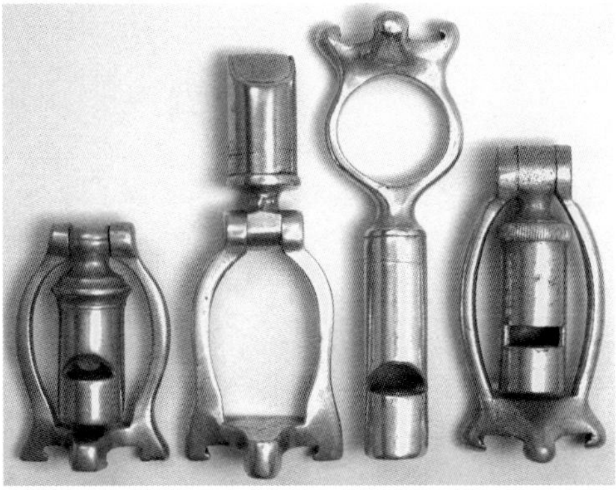

J HUDSON & CO

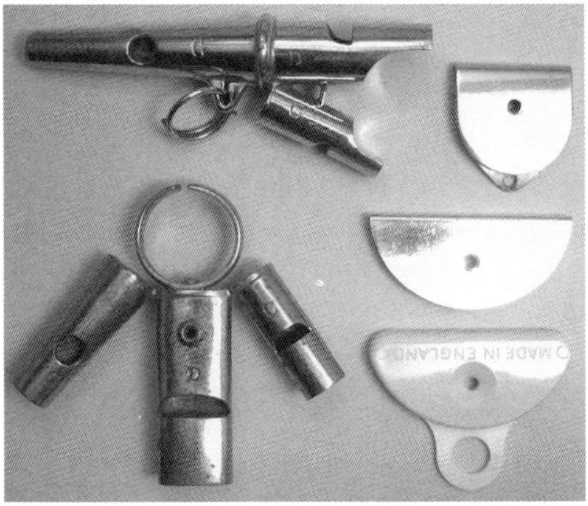

Left: *J Hudson & Co shepherds' dog whistles. Clockwise from top left; triple call marked 'G', 'D', 'C' for Go, Down & Come, late 1930s with winged 'V' ring fitting, length 95mm; mouth whistle, nickel silver, 1940s; mouth whistle, aluminium, 1960s; mouth whistle, bite-resistant plastic, 1990s; The Fletcher (designed by a Scottish shepherd of that name), Marked 'G', 'D', 'C' for Go Down & Come, the 'D' whistle having a stop-hole, 1930s-40s.*

Left & right: *J Hudson & Co nickel silver 12-gauge cartridge extractor. Extractors may be confirmed as being made by Husons by checking that the 'footprint' of the claw (right) is absolutely identical with that shown, however, the '12' may be in a different place. Rare.*

Right: *J Hudson & Co 'Galton' silent dog whistle. Named after Sir Francis Galton (1822-1911) who designed a high-pitched whistle after discovering some animals could hear beyond the human range. Left; 2nd model with short mouthpiece – the 1st model, launched in 1935, had no locking nut above the body, nor a drilled knop to take a split ring. Centre left; 3rd model with long mouthpiece (a feature of all later patterns) next to its carrying case. Centre right; 4th model with integral case marked 'Acme England Pat. No.486417', the patent was valid from 1936 to 1950, after that date no number appears on the whistle. In modern examples the metal fipple is replaced by a plastic one.*

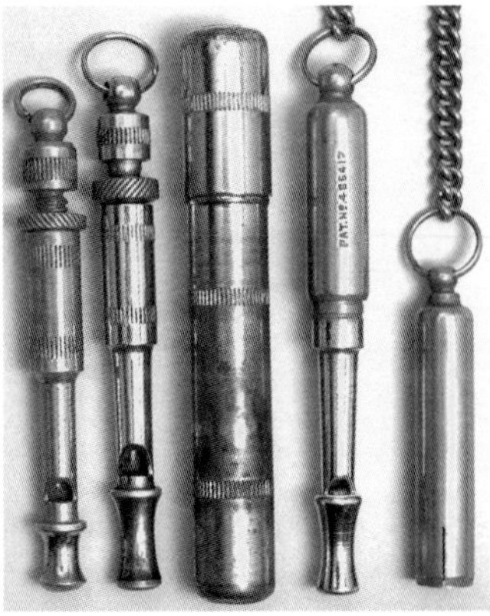

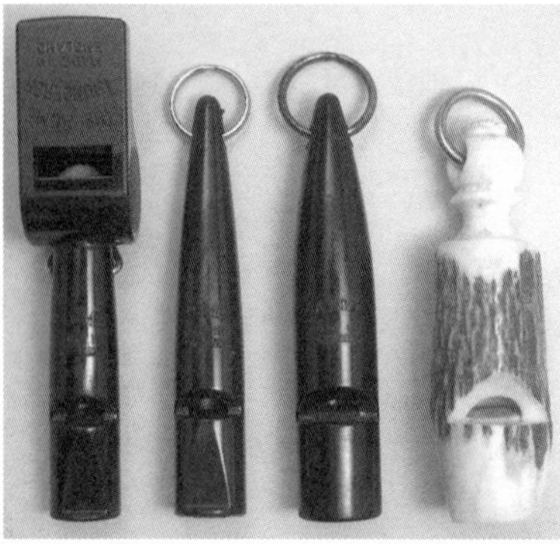

J Hudson & Co dog whistles made to a standard pitch. Replacing a lost whistle with one identical in pitch avoids the need to retrain a dog to a different sounding one. Other modern fixed-pitched plastic calls not illustrated include models 210 and 210½. Left; model 642, made from a model 211½ combined with 'The Acme Thunderer', length 92mm, from 1991 onwards. Centre left; 211½ model 1990s. Centre right; 211½ model, a larger whistle than the previous example, but made to the same pitch, 1970s. Right; fixed-pitch staghorn whistle, 1950s.

DOG & KENNEL WHIPS

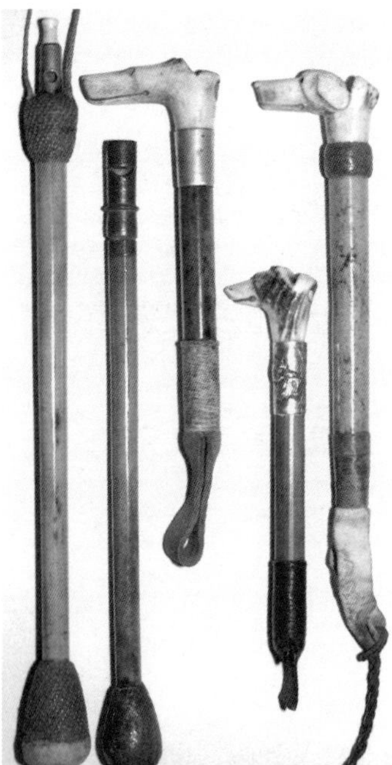

Left: *Dog & kennel crops/whips. Left to right; weighted cane with J Dixon & Sons Beaufort whistle with bone mouthpiece, late 19th century, length 415mm; weighted cane with Britannia metal whistle; staghorn dog's-head whistle, nickel silver band, 'M H Mason Maker London'; staghorn dog's-head whistle, nickel silver band depicting a fox with a game bird in its mouth; staghorn dog's-head whistle.*

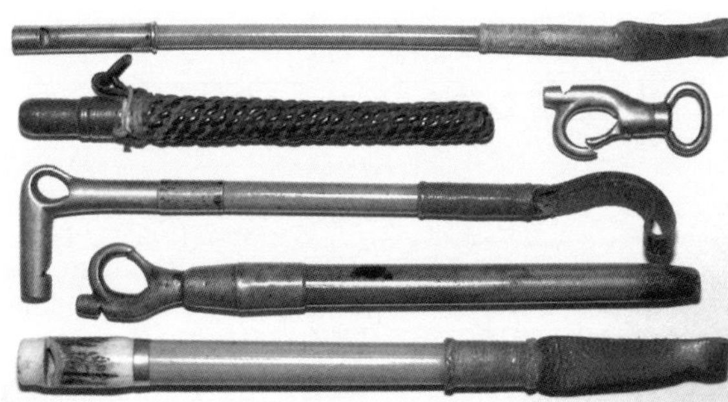

Above: *Dog & kennel crops. Top to bottom; silver whistle, Chester 1896, length 310mm; Britannia metal whistle designed for attaching to a whip; whistle with latch, leather strap missing; whistle with latch, silver band marked 'Swaine'; whistle with latch, end of cane missing; staghorn whistle with silver band marked 'Brigg London', 1922 hallmarks.*

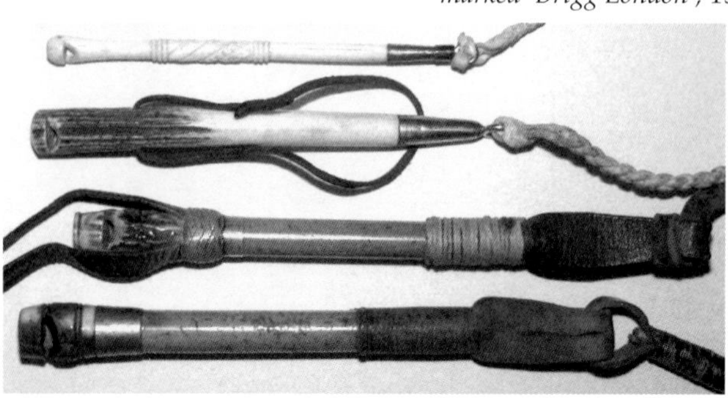

Dog & kennel whips. Top to bottom; carved bone whistle with silver plated fitting for whip attachment, length 200mm; staghorn whistle with nickel silver fitting; staghorn whistle, with silver fittings marked 'Swaine & Adeney London', 1906 hallmarks; staghorn whistle with nickel silver band.

Miscellaneous whistles

Illustrated are calls whose design precludes them from being included elsewhere.

Left: *Bent & Parker double note call, 'The "New Borough" Whistle Osborne & Son New St Birmm', the end of the body marked 'Patent No.10828', nickel silver, 1894-1908.*

Right: *A De Courcy & Co. Left; cyclist's spherical whistle with spoked wheel design to sides, diameter 26mm, rare. Right; 'Boy Scouts', flat whistle with stop-hole, late 19th to early 20th century, rare.*

Left: *G & J W Hawksley nickel silver call marked with the maker's name, late 19th to early 20th century, length 41mm, rare.*

Above: *James Dixon & Sons Swiss/French railways pattern whistle, diameter of ball 24mm, late 19th century, rare.*

Left: *J Hudson & Co sports whistle with finger-ring. Engraved into the Bakelite 'M Neal Hockey & Net Ball 1938'.*

Right: *J Hudson & Co. Top & centre; Swiss/French railways pattern call. Largest ball diameter 26mm, late 1940s-50s. Bottom; Spherical call, diameter 26mm, late 19th to early 20th century. All rare.*

Below: *J Hudson & Co. Top; referee's pencil holder whistle with an ivorine writing tablet, late 1920s, length without pencil 100mm, very rare. This example has a much worn tablet, original size about 55x35mm. Centre; 'Acme Redg Made in England', flat vest pocket pattern with stop-hole, 1950s. Bottom; Mauser bullet pattern, 'Policia De La Capital' on reverse, 1900s, rare.*

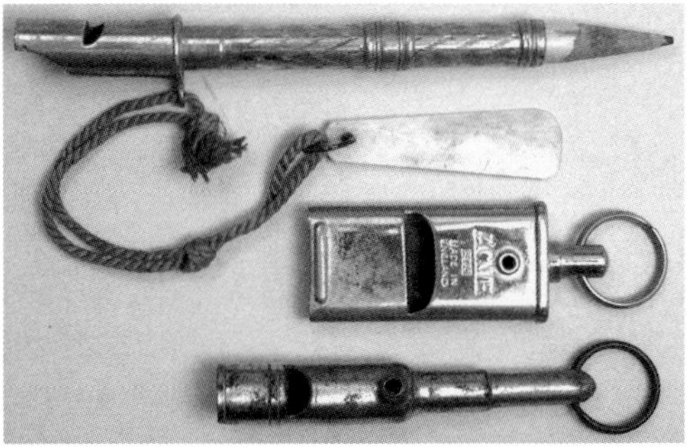

Below: *Stevens & Son brass bell whistles with ivory mouthpieces, early 19th century to pre-1871. Left to right; length 72mm; length 77mm; 'West London', believed to be West London Railway; 'Stevens & Son Southwark'. All very rare.*

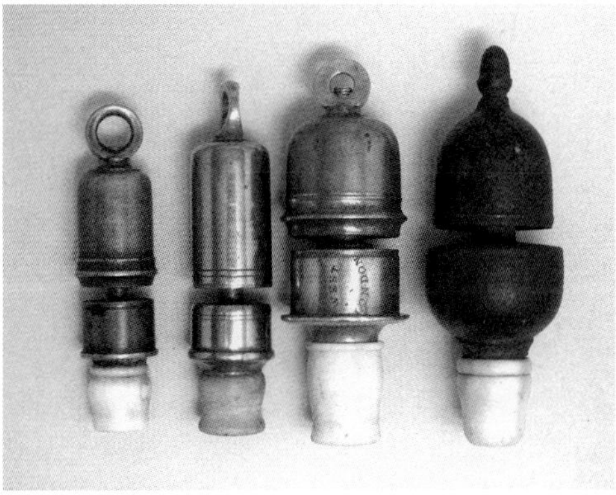

Sirens

Below are considered J Hudson & Co's Model 147 sirens and their derivatives. Sound is produced by air escaping through the holes of a rotating perforated wheel, the rotor, and the pitch varies with the speed of rotation.

Hudsons registered a design for a case to take a siren in 1895, number 250010 which had ten vents at the top. Their patent for a siren mechanism dates from 1907, number 24900 which also allows for the attachment of a horn. All the sirens that the author has examined with ten vents have the cases marked 'Patent' leaving a mystery as to what siren was originally combined with the Registered Design case. In the 2000s sirens are still made in nickel plated brass but in previous years they have also been made in silver plated brass, hallmarked silver and gold. In addition they could be combined with a general service whistle, fitted with a finger grip at the back, or attached to a pigskin or leather wristlet, Patent 25619/1907. They were also fitted to double-action hand pumps for motorists' or yachtsmen's use, and with a rubber bulb and bracket for cyclists.

Two inexpensive patterns were produced in the mid 1950s. In one the mouthpiece was crimped to an open tube containing the mechanism, and the other simply had the end of the tube flattened to form a mouthpiece.

In the 1910s huge mouth sirens were built, 126mm long. The Wynn Mark I Message Carrying Rocket of 1917 was fitted with its mechanism together with smoke and flare producing powder, to indicate its passage through the air.

Above: *c.1907. Top open, no vents, rare.*

Above *c.1908*

Above: *Left; mid 1910s. Right; c.1921.*

Right: *Left; early 1950s. Right; 1990s.*

Below: *J Hudson & Co sirens. Top: attached to a pigskin wristlet, stamped 'Patent 25619 1907'. Used by WWI motorcycle despatch riders. Sirens with wristlets do not have a top fitting. Length overall 245mm, late 1900s to early 1910s. Bottom; huge siren, 126mm, rare, 1910s. The mechanism was used in the Wynn Rocket.*

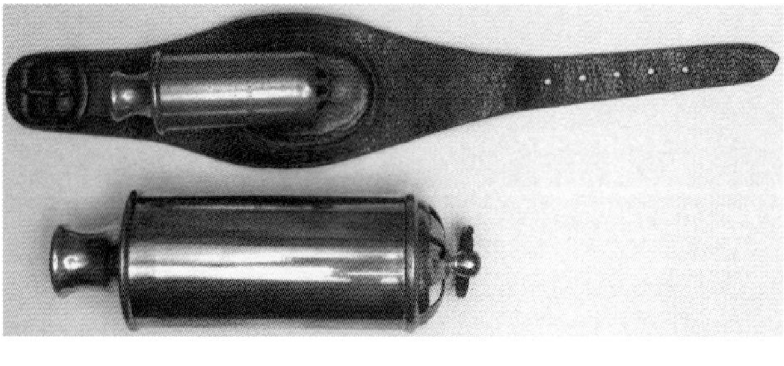

DATING J HUDSON & CO SIRENS

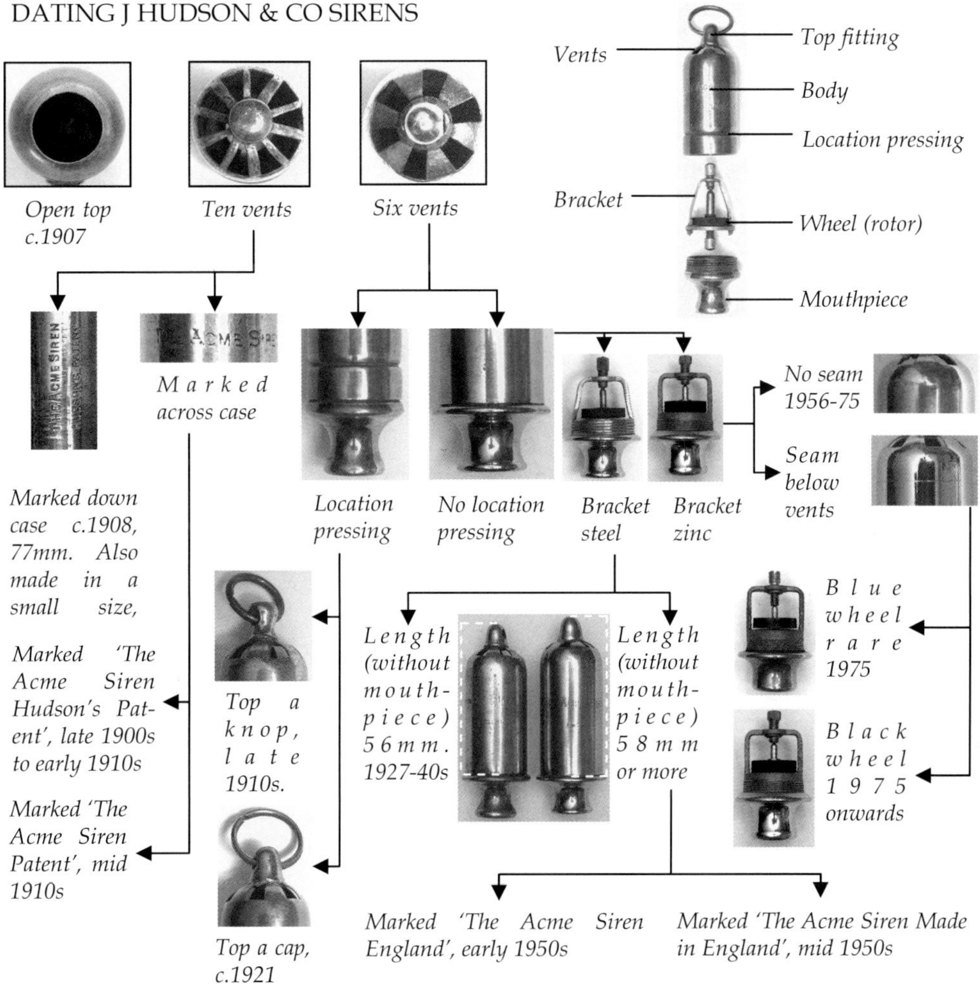

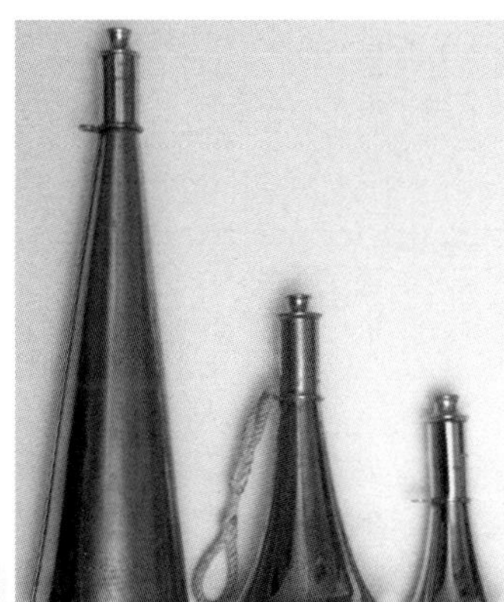

Right: *J Hudson & Co siren horns. Made for many years. Left; 330mm, late 1900s to early 1910s. Centre; 182mm, 1970s. Right; 125mm, mid 1950s to mid 1970s. A 605mm model was also made.*

Below: *Wynn Mark I Message Carrying Rocket, 1917. The mechanism from the huge Hudson siren illustrated on the previous page was fitted at the front. The rocket has a hollow central section with a wire message holder, a piece of paper and a pencil, and it has light and smoke emitting powder. On the front could be fitted three different brass flanges which increased wind resistance, thus governing the distance travelled.*

The manufacturers

Trade directories from the 'Golden Age' of whistle making, 1860s-1930s, have listed many different manufacturers over the years. Many of the small makers have left no trace of their products and little advertising matter. Notwithstanding these minor drawbacks, nearly all whistles that the collector comes across are identifiable. Many of those that are unmarked can be identified by their design characteristics. However, probably there will always be a few whistles that defy accurate and positive identification. Some makers (for example Auld, De Courcy, Hudson) have supplied calls marked in such a way as to suggest the customer was also the maker of the whistle. The true manufacturer of any such whistle can usually be determined from the call's specific features.

ADIE BROTHERS, BIRMINGHAM. Manufacturing silversmiths of Soho Hill, who made radar and aircraft parts during the 1939-45 conflict. They made nickel plated brass whistles in 1940 and 1941.

SAMUEL AULD, GLASGOW. Brass founders, plumbers, gas fitters, bell hangers, polishers and whistle manufacturers. They were at Gallowgate in the 1880s, Wood Lane in 1900 and Cowcaddens in 1903. In 1907 J Hudson & Co purchased their whistle making tools and stock.

B & H WHISTLES, BIRMINGHAM. In the late 1960s William Hussy left J Hudson & Co to establish B & H Whistles. He sold out to M Y Dart Co in 1972.

JOHN BARRALL, BIRMINGHAM. A whistle maker between 1886 and 1898 whose early whistles were fundamental in manufacture but which became increasingly more accomplished.

BENT & PARKER, BIRMINGHAM. An important company making military accoutrements and whistles. They competed for the first contract to supply the Metropolitan Police with whistles in 1884.

BLACK & CO, GLASGOW. They made escargot whistles marked 'McPherson Brothers Maker' for resale by that company until 1898. The records of the period list more than one Black & Co but it is thought the company was situated in Frederick Street and were packing case makers, zinc and tin workers.

CASCELLOID LTD, LEICESTER. Founded by A E Pallett in Leicester in 1919. The company made toys from celluloid and plastic. In 1985 the name 'Palitoy' was dropped.

CONEY & CO, BIRMINGHAM. A manufacturer of nut crackers, corkscrews, steel toys and whistles at Lionel Street. Their whistles date from the late nineteenth to early twentieth century.

A DE COURCY & CO, BIRMINGHAM. Founded by Alfred De Courcy in 1888 who left J Hudson & Co to start on his own. He was of Irish descent, and a talented engineer and innovative designer who patented several whistles. J Hudson & Co bought his whistle business in 1927, but he continued making publican's sundries and beer tankards until his death in 1931.

J DIXON & SONS, SHEFFIELD. Founded in 1804. Manufacturers of sporting tackle, silver goods, Sheffield and electro plate, Britannia metal and nickel silver. In the

1880s the company was a world leader in the manufacture of shooting accessories. They made high quality whistles from at least the 1840s. Their trade mark is a depiction of a valveless trumpet from which is hanging a banner. In 1947 the company took over G & J W Hawksley.

WILLIAM DOWLER & SONS, BIRMINGHAM. A long-established company manufacturing many goods including military insignia, badges, accoutrements and whistles. In c.1904 they abandoned whistle making, sub-contracting orders to J Hudson & Co and A De Courcy & Co. A few years earlier, in 1901, the company moved from Great Charles Street to Graham Street. Whistles with the later address need to be checked as to which company actually made them, by inspecting the internal components. Dowler would loan their out punches to Hudson and De Courcy to produce the markings required on whistles' bodies.

J R GAUNT & SONS, BIRMINGHAM. A manufacturing company which has been making military ornaments since 1750. They devised a patent design in 1911, number 22309, for making escargots, Beauforts, general service and round whistles essentially from two metal stampings soldered together. No whistles made to this patent have been identified.

G & J W HAWKSLEY, SHEFFIELD. Founded in 1840. A manufacturer of gun implements, shooting accessories, cutlery, and golf bags. Their trade mark is a bird holding an envelope with the word, 'Despatch'. They sold their own whistles and those made Dixons and Hudsons.

HILLIARD & THOMASON, BIRMINGHAM. John Hilliard and John Thomason were silversmiths in partnership from 1847. They made small goods including caddy spoons, tapersticks and knife handles. They were particularly known for their bosuns' calls and they also made other patterns of whistles.

J HUDSON & CO, BIRMINGHAM. Established in 1870 at 17 St Mark's Street, in 1883 at 84 Buckingham Street, in 1885 at 131 Barr Street, in 1888 at 13 Barr Street, and finally from 1909 onwards at 244 Barr Street. Joseph Hudson learnt his trade at Bent & Parker in the 1860s, earning extra income by repairing shoes. In 1870 Joseph Hudson, aged 22, was in partnership with his brother James, aged 20. James died in 1889, Joseph in 1930. J Hudson & Co have made other products besides whistles including; animal calls, alberts, leather belts, castanets, violin accessories, button sticks, truncheons and badges. They also purchased whistles and goods manufactured by other companies for resale by themselves. In October 1940 the premises were hit by a high explosive bomb which exploded in the basement causing disruption to production. The proprietor, Clifford Hudson did not entirely recover from the shock of this incident. In the 2000s Hudsons continue to make a range of whistles in both metal and plastic.

B LILLY & SONS, BIRMINGHAM. Located in Barr Street in the early 20th century. They manufactured and bought in whistles for re-sale from De Courcy, Yates, Ward and probably other makers.

J LINEGAR, BIRMINGHAM. Located at 63-4 Spencer Street in the 1880s.

PETER MCDONALD, GLASGOW. He was active in 1890 and had a business association with H A Ward of Birmingham.

MCPHERSON BROTHERS, GLASGOW. Hardware merchants, ironmongers and dealers in guns and tackle. Whistles marked 'McPherson Brothers Makers' were made by Black & Co, and J Hudson & Co.

M Y DART CO, BARNET. The company bought out W Hussy's whistle business, B & H Whistles, in 1972.

ROBERT PRINGLE & SONS, MIDDLESEX. Formed in 1825 by Robert Pringle, a working jeweller, at the Wilderness Works, Clerkenwell Road. Pringle's trademark, No.26839 of September 1881, was a circle within which was 'WW' and crossed axes. In the mid 1960s the company stopped manufacturing jewellery and silverware.

RUDD BROS, BIRMINGHAM. Stampers, piercers, tin toy and inexpensive whistle makers of Abbey Street. They were active from the 1900s to 1930s.

H W SHORT, LONDON. A scientific instrument maker of Seven Sisters Road, who made very few high quality two-piece whistles.

J SIMMONS, BIRMINGHAM. Whistles marked 'Jas Simmons Maker' were made by J Hudson & Co.

SMITH & WRIGHT, BIRMINGHAM. A manufacturer of small metal goods. It is believed that as well as making their own whistles, some were made for them by W Dowler & Sons.

STADIUM LTD, BIRMINGHAM. Motor car accessories manufacturer who briefly made military whistles dated 1941.

J STEVENS & SONS, LONDON & GLASGOW. A company who manufactured many goods including; railway signals, iron bridges, signalmens' houses, turnstiles and ships' signal lanterns. They were gas fitters, brass founders, hydraulic engineers and high quality whistle makers from at least the 1840s, supplying the military and the railways. Believed to be the designers of the almost-spherical Porteous top for general service whistles. J Hudson & Co made whistles for them in the early 1900s.

THOMAS SYKES, SHEFFIELD. The company is famous for powder flasks, especially their patent of 1814. Whistles marked 'Sykes' were probably made by J Dixon & Sons.

RICHARD A WALTON, BIRMINGHAM. A one-time foreman of J Hudson & Co who established the short-lived Universal Whistle Works in 1898, selling out to Hudsons in 1904.

HENRY A WARD, BIRMINGHAM. Active from c.1889 to 1908 from various addresses including the Alpha Gun Works, Weasman Street. He had a business association with P McDonald, Glasgow.

C T WILLETTS, BIRMINGHAM. Traded from Heneage Street as steel toy, nutcracker, corkscrew and whistle maker.

THOMAS YATES, BIRMINGHAM. In Coleshill Street and manufacturers from the early nineteenth century of a large range of goods including spirit flasks, picnic baskets, sandwich boxes, spoons, ladles, and a range of knobs, tops, handles, knife rests and cruets. They were probably the leading manufacturers of whistles for most of the nineteenth century. They manufactured over 125 different whistles in various alloys with production ceasing in the early twentieth century.

Glossary & trademarks

Auld-type whistles. Whistles with a window design similar to those by S Auld. A convenient way of classifying some round whistles.

Backstamp. The markings on the underside of a whistle.

Barrel. The resonating chamber of an escargot whistle.

Barrel-end. Not a separate component, but that part of a complex metal blank which becomes the end of an escargot's barrel.

Beaufort whistle. A conical, or tapered tube, whistle with two windows, blown through the smallest end. Beaufort whistles for military use have a single window and fipple mouthpiece.

Black oxidation. A mixture into which a whistle is placed to give it an all-over black finish. It is not a lacquer but a chemically produced finish.

Britannia metal. An alloy, similar to pewter, mostly of tin with antimony and copper. It is shiny when new but can oxydise to a dull finish. Once dull it cannot be polished back to the original shine. Can be electroplated.

Call. Another name for a whistle.

Composite whistle. A pattern made up of two or more calls joined together.

Diaphragm. The metal component inside the whistle immediately below the window. Usually a disc or a wedge.

End-cap. The disc-shaped component which is soldered to the sides of an escargot's barrel.

Escargot whistle. A whistle when viewed from the side is reminiscent of a snail.

Finger grip. A metal fitting attached to the back of escargots through which fingers may be placed to hold the whistle.

Finger ring. A metal fitting attached to the back of a general service whistle which will pass over a gloved finger.

Fipple. The plug which forms the back of the mouthpiece of a round whistle and directs the breath to the edge of the window.

General service whistle (GSW). A whistle shaped as a cylindrical tube with two windows, often referred to as a police whistle even if not issued to the police.

German silver. Another name for nickel silver.

Glasgow escargot. One of the two styles of escargots, see page five.

Knop. An almost spherical top fitting above the top-cap, a knob.

London escargot. One of the two styles of escargots, see page five.

Loop. A top fitting to which can be attached a ring to take a lanyard.

Nickel silver. An alloy of nickel, zinc and copper. It contains no silver.

Overlabel. A plate soldered to a whistle, either blank or marked. Often used to cover up unwanted markings.

Pewter. An alloy of tin and lead that cannot be plated. Now often used to describe an alloy of tin, copper, antimony and/or bismuth.

Pillar top. A pillar-like fitting at the top of a whistle.

Police whistle. A name often used to describe a general service whistle which may, or may not, have been issued to the police.

Porteous top. An almost spherical top fitted to some general service whistles.

Side plates. Additional plates fixed to the sides of escargot whistles as a strengthening measure.

Stop-hole. A hole in the body of a whistle over which a finger may be placed to produce a second note.

Tine. A prong, like that of a fork, that projects from a diaphragm at rightangles. It is designed to add mechanical strength and was the subject of J Hudson & Co's first patent of 1885. The first whistles issued to the Metropolitan Police bearing Hudson's 84 Buckingham Street address did not have this feature and the vast majority needed repairing due to diaphragm failure.

Tooth-grip. A raised part or pressing, or added metal strip, at the front of a whistle aiding its retention in the mouth.

Tongue. A Glasgow escargot component fixed to the inside bottom of the mouthpiece and curving down into the barrel. Its function is to prevent the 'pea' jamming.

Top-cap. The component at the top of a whistle above which is the loop or knop.

Top loop. The very top of a whistle to which a ring or lanyard may be attached.

Under-strengthening. An additional strip of metal added to some London escargots, especially button whistles. The strip emerges from the front of the mouthpiece and curves down towards the barrel where it is soldered.

White metal. Casting metal generally.

Window. The opening in a whistle's body from which the sound emanates.

Wiring. The method of holding the various whistle components together by wire during manufacture prior to soldering. The groove in the top fitting frequently found on Hudson's escargots was designed to aid the wiring process.

J HUDSON & CO TRADEMARKS

TRADEMARK	YEAR
Acme	1927
Acme City	1907
Acme Referee	1908
Acmeoid	1914
Emca	1922
The Acme	1886
The Acme Boy Scouts	1909
The Kinglet	1907
The Metropolitan	1884
Thunderer	1927